The Secret Laws Of Narcissistic Abuse

21 Psychological Weapons to Read the Mind and Counter Manipulate a Narcissist, even if your're an Empath plagued by Codependency

I0414812

Table of Contents

Introduction

Most people have been at the wrong end of narcissistic manipulation. After going through it, the victim of this abuse is left spent, feeling guilty, undesirable and confused. This is especially dire for those who are empaths, worse still for the empaths who grew up with narcissistic parents. This is one of the foundations of codependency.

Narcissists are incredibly competent at their game, and what makes a great target for them are some of the things that we are proudest of. Essentially, they target the good-natured for they know that they will listen, and when the narcissists know they have an ear, the games begin.

People who have excellent boundaries are virtually immune to this: they know how to interrupt manipulation attempts before they can cause any damage. They know that no one needs to borrow their phone and that it should stay in their pocket. They know that if someone wants to be close to you within minutes, days, or weeks, then something is definitely wrong. They can smell the desperation and they know how to avoid it. Empaths do not.

In their world there is no getting the best of people. Empaths assume, and want to believe in, the authenticity of the experience of being alive. They extend to others what they want to be extended to themselves. The narcissist cues into this and takes what the empath is willing to extend, but offers nothing of the like in return.

This book details 21 Laws of the experience of being exposed to a narcissist. It will show you how much you stand to lose by leaving yourself undefended, and it will lead you towards better ways of living. Remember that we are our own centers.

To help clarify the terms used in this book, please consult this list of definitions:

- Narcissism is included in the Cluster B Personality Disorders, the dramatic, emotional, and erratic cluster. A narcissist is a person obsessed with themselves. This can manifest in overt and covert expressions. Narcissists are obsessed about the perception people have of them and will manipulate others in order to extract their attention. Their condition of uncaringness will not abate with time, the disorder has no cure. They are real people with real feelings, but they are also dangerous.

- Overt narcissism is the more pronounced version of the disorder. They openly show hostility and manipulate through fear. Often through control over living circumstances, they corner their victims.

- A covert narcissist is difficult to read. They often are withdrawn and hard to get to know, presenting themselves as a sensitive type. This front allows them to appear as a caring person so that they can sneak into the lives of their victims, and then manipulate them through conniving means. They will never admit to their actions. Instead they insist that they're being underappreciated or otherwise treated poorly.

- Highly Sensitive People, or HSPs, are people who chemically react to the world differently. It is estimated that between 15-20% of the population are HSPs. They are people who react to stimuli in a more exaggerated way, and they are people who release less dopamine. This means they are more prone to stress, but also more prone to focus. They are exposed to all stimuli, positive and negative, in a more heightened sense than the common person.

- Empaths are a category of HSP, and they are an estimated 2-3% of the population. There are many categories of HSP. The empath is defined by an increased sensitivity to the emotions of the surrounding people. They are often more drawn into the experiences of others and fictional stories, than they are to their own lives.

- Narcissistic supply is what every narcissist desires to turn their targets into. It is a state of being which a narcissist forces a person into which allows the narcissists to draw resources from the victim freely. These resources can be time, attention, money, ideas, or anything else that can be possessed. They convert their victim into a source for the resources they most desire.

When dealing with narcissists, empaths and HSP, it's important to understand these definitions. To misidentify someone as a narcissist is an awful thing because you will misinterpret someone as a predator. This isn't the worst thing to do, but it is similar to what narcissists do to their victims. It's best to avoid it and seriously consider your situation.

Exposure to a narcissist will leave you feeling hollow. You will feel bad being around them without explanation. They will always be late. The questions you ask won't be answered. You will be taken advantage of repeatedly. You will be lied to. You will develop brain fog, making it more difficult to think, more difficult to remember. It will be an awful influence on your life.

Not all of these conditions need to be met for there to be proof of the influence of a narcissist in your life, and perhaps not everybody who engages in this behavior is a narcissist, but they're common symptoms of a problem.

This book often uses the relationship between empaths and narcissists as a model for narcissistic abuse because empaths are naturally attractive targets to turn into narcissistic supply. Through being Highly Sensitive People, and especially through being HSPs with a social nature, they are vulnerable to being taken advantage of due to their good nature. By taking advantage of this natural desire to help others, narcissists can coax empaths into converting into perpetually productive systems of supply.

The relationship between empaths and narcissists is used not because they are the only people that can be affected by narcissistic abuse. Narcissists can and will target everybody, so even if you are a 'normal' person you may be deeply affected by the influence of a narcissist in your life.

What puts empaths at risks are features that every person can relate to. Empaths and narcissists are not inhuman, but exaggerations of natural tendencies. Everybody has a connection to others and everybody had a sense of self. The empath's nature is a dramatized version of our sense to help our fellow person, wanting to warm them in the cold and assist them when they're sick. An empath feels this connection to an extreme degree, dedicating their lives to serving the need that they feel to give back to the people around them. This leads them to often develop a poor sense of self and a poor sense of independence.

The narcissist's disorder stems from the opposite experience. Instead of centering on a sense for others, their condition centers on a sense of self. This may seem easy to look down on, as selfish is an insult within our very language, but that misunderstands the situation. Narcissists aren't villains, they're people who are trying to survive, and as it appears to them, manipulating the world around them seems to be the best way to live the lives that they want to.

Often narcissists have grandiose missions of healing others. Many want to open schools, or contribute to charities, or otherwise improve the world around them. One must understand these conditions are not black and white; there are many caring and giving narcissists, as there are many cruel and conniving empaths. They are special cases, but they do exist. These labels do not mean good and bad, but they do describe archetypes that the human psyche is attracted to falling into. The reason we discuss them together is that they give us a good portrait of human relationships in general, not because they are an inflexible paradigm that everything falls under.

Anyone can be affected by a narcissist. This book's aim is to teach how to break free from narcissistic influence. It will use these terms to further identify the patterns of narcissistic behavior and how to heal from its influence.

To reverse engineer narcissism, play their game.

Put yourself first.

Law 1

«Do Not Forget What You Meant»

The Law of Projection

The primary tool, the broken boundary that is the missing brick which lets narcissists in, is projection. It's a cruel, indirect manipulation tactic that cues into one of the most venerable virtues in the empath: their ability to listen.

Projection takes that willingness to believe and runs it for all that it is worth. When you're engaged to a narcissist, you will find yourself at fault for many things you can't remember doing. This is because you didn't do them. They told you that you did, and you believed them.

Lies are the rule, not the exception with narcissists. They will find ways to bend the littlest things to their advantage. Inconsequential things, such as how fast they can drink a bottle of water, are not small enough for a narcissist to ignore. They will abuse of any opportunity to gain social standing or reputation.

Without hesitation, they will manipulate your trust. Often, they will take credit for good ideas and blame bad ideas on you no matter who came up with them.

This is because, although they are drowning in shame, they cannot process it. If they were to do so, they would be hit with such a wave of self-hate that they would be sick. Narcissists are disgusted by what they are.

When narcissists run into complicated feelings that they don't have the tool-set to deal with, they outsource. They look for people who know how to deal with it. They look for healers. Once they have found them, they corner them and then drink from their healing energies greedily. This is how they turn empaths and Highly Sensitive People into narcissistic supply.

Narcissists look for a pincushion for all of the negativity in their life when they hunt for supply. If you are unfortunate enough to be born into a narcissist household, then there is a likelihood you became the scapegoat of the family. They blamed their own failures on you, economic and social; they convinced you that you were amoral and ungrateful. That is all too common in the narcissistic home. This guilt is shoved on to you because the abuser doesn't want to hold onto it himself.

As a spouse, the abuse is similarly inescapable. The difference is instead of being their responsibility you're their measure of sexual self-worth, how they identify how well they're doing. You're a trophy. If you have a blemish or a scar, then they obsess over it as a direct reflection of their value. Unsatisfied with that much, they will then also load their own flaws onto you, and criticize their own lifestyles through you.

Their dependency on you as the medium in which they process negative energy and thoughts may become overbearing or obsessive. Without blaming you for their own issues, they may become agitated or more insecure. This often creates a sense of guilt in the target of their abuse, causing them to stay so that the narcissist doesn't get worse.

However, for Highly Sensitive People, or empaths, this relationship creates a completely false image. The narcissist benefits heavily because HSPs are brilliant at processing emotional energy, so the narcissist gets to wash all of their thoughts for free, but the HSPs becomes filthy in the process. They become loaded with guilt and hate for things they never did.

This distraction is ultimately harmful to everybody involved. It wears away at the target of the projection, throwing their sense of reality into question, but it also prevents the narcissist from honestly addressing their lives and becoming mature enough to grow from the issues that face.

According to your lover, you can never go out and have a good time. You ask if there is any difference between the two of you, or if there is anything you can do, but the questions lead nowhere other than yes, you can do something. There's something about you, your attitude. It follows you two everywhere, like a stench. If something doesn't change, he doesn't know how much longer he can handle it.

Yet the last time you went for coffee it was him who was talking back at the barista, insisting that the coffee was off, that she burned it. He was the one looking around at everybody's face, saying how stupid they looked, how *simple.* He was the reason you stopped hanging out with that friend, and the other one, and eventually all of them over the years. He was the one who hated everything. You just wanted to take a step out to appreciate the city. How was it your fault?

Still, you try, you're always trying. You show him a new place in town, some brunch spot you could try out that weekend. Begrudgingly he agrees to do it, but he has a negative posture while doing so. His shoulders are slumped, his eyes are dark, and his voice heavy. There's not much faith in him.

Sunday comes and you go out. The weather is beautiful and the restaurant is in an adorable part of town. You find a table near the window and the light comes in crisply over the interior. You sit down and look through the menu. Most of it is medium fare, not too pricey, but still quality.

You order your meal; he gets the same thing as you. The conversation never picks up despite several attempts by you to get it going. Mostly it's a standoffish silence between you two as he looks anywhere but at you, studying the décor of the restaurant, the other patrons, and the scene outside. He makes comments about the crowd being too uppity. You smile.

The food comes and it's amazing. The presentation is tasteful, it smells delicious, and it's cooked so well that it falls apart in your mouth. His first reaction is to complain about the portions, then comment on how plain everything tastes.

Unsurprisingly, the second half of the meal follows the same pattern of uncomfortable quips and indirect statements. By the end of it, you don't even feel like walking around town, you pay the bill, get back in the car, and go home.

A week later, he brings up how great that restaurant was. He says he was happy you went out to it, wishing only that you felt better that day. More than anything you want to scream, but you try to hold the conversation. Twice he implies that he was actually the one who suggested you went out to that part of town, to that restaurant. Again, he comments on your mood and wishes you could be out in public without feeling so stilted.

Half of you wants to go out on a date with someone else just to prove how normal you can talk, how this standard of conversation isn't everybody's. The other half of you wants to move far away and hide in a cabin buried in the snow. Instead of doing either, you suffer his delusions either in silence or while crying. Every time you try to correct him, he fights back viciously, so you've learned that it's not okay to stand your ground.

The risk of allowing this energy in your life is to lose trust in your inner voice. You won't be able to hear yourself, to differentiate between what you think is real and what you think is fake. You won't be able to find yourself in the mirror.

There is no way to defend yourself from projection or reverse it while preserving the relationship. It will wither and die once you stick up for yourself in almost every situation, and if you are fighting for your health, it should. The narcissist will not be interested in preying on you once his influence is not complete. They thrive on controlling thoughts and manipulating trust. Once they realize they've lost the power to do so they start hunting for another victim.

What you need to do to defeat this tactic is the truth, to know it, to stick by it, and to be able to confide in yourself about it. You must be able to identify what is objectively true in your situation, what is happening, and why. This may be difficult to do because of the emotions that surround the situation, especially if they are intimate, but with patience and a willingness to be neutral, the truth will surface. In this situation, writing down how you feel and why you feel that way may help you keep track of your feelings. A journal might be the thing you need to start identifying which of your feelings are being negatively manipulated.

Luckily, the narcissist will give you the truth with clarity if you read them. Once you can recognize their behavior you can see their thoughts being externalized, because the shame they apply to you is actually their shame, and the guilt they try to shift onto you is really their own.

To identify this behavior, remember all the criticisms that the narcissist has given you, which made you feel awful because you couldn't imagine yourself doing that. The reason it feels so awful is that it is a mischaracterization of you. That is the projection, when someone tries to force their personality over your own. This is because they can't truly perceive other people; they perceive people as the ideas they have of them.

Once you can realize this, you will be given the map to their subconscious. Their way of coping with the things inside of themselves they don't want to admit is to shove it onto other people. They will apply all of their negative attributes and inner thoughts to everything around them, as they rarely have the presence of mind to meaningfully criticize things outside of themselves.

Do not allow this energy into your consciousness. That negativity is not your own and you will not benefit from it, nor from the narcissist. Their projection of self-hate can only spread more negativity. Keep it outside of yourself because if you don't it will only cause harm.

For empaths, this dynamic is especially difficult due to the empath's tendency to believe. They never want to assert their own point of view over others; they prefer to share authority with the rest of humanity. The narcissist takes advantage of this and uses that trust to lead the empath into thinking that the negative attributes of the narcissist are the empath's qualities, blaming them for everything the narcissist is ashamed of. This supplies the narcissist with a scapegoat and drains the empath of any energy to fight back.

You must stand up to the narcissist and define yourself. Do not let them do it for you, or else you will quickly become a shadow of them. Remember what you believe, what you're interested in, and your principles. Keep true to them and don't let yourself be told that they don't matter.

Law 2

«Do Not Believe What You Are Told You Said»

The Law of Gaslighting

Over time, the narcissist tries to corner every perspective. He wants to dominate every conversation, every decision, and every thought. Eventually, he will snake his way into acting as the checks and balances of whatever he can get a hold of. Gaslighting is another one of the key tools in the narcissist's tool-set that they use to attain their goals.

In his perception it's not that the world runs on its own axis, it's that there is a truth and he knows it. In intimate relationships, he will slowly try to rise to the place of arbiter of reality. He will want the final say in how things are remembered.

This is because he is trying to secure a position from which to manipulate. Narcissists require dominance over perception because it allows them to do more with less effort. To manipulate physically is difficult, such as using someone's taste in food to get them to go out at a certain time every week. It is much easier to use your words to convince others. The narcissist prefers that angle, to be able to lie without question. By insisting on certain perceptions of reality, they open up opportunities in their life that they don't deserve.

A common reason why they use this tactic is to conceal abuse. By being in control of how things are remembered, they can insist on things having not happened, or the intentions that were at play.

Instead of allowing you to have a voice in why you acted how you acted, they assume to know what your true motivations were.

This dynamic is especially worrisome for empaths because it is one of the strongest bonds in codependent relationships. Empaths spend their entire life listening to other people, so doubt is a natural part of their experience. The narcissist preys on this attribute and convince the empath to fall unhealthily far into that doubt, encouraging the empath to question their perception of reality. This is advantageous for the narcissist because an unstable psyche is easier to manipulate. They are invested in the instability of their target because it allows them to lie to them further and, possibly, extract more resources.

Unfortunately for the empath, the narcissist's confidence will be intoxicating, like poison. The insistence of the narcissist leads most victims to give in and let their lives be rewritten. Empaths rarely tend towards conflict, so continually having to defend their perspective quickly becomes tiring and many don't have the energy to keep it up for long.

This is how empaths end up converted into narcissistic supply. If they do not spend the time defending their own positions and perspectives from the narcissist's advances then they get lost in his lies. One of the most common symptoms of gaslighting is brain fog, which compounds the issue of preserving your identity after being targeted by one.

Many more issues stem from this form of abuse because it is an attack on the victim's sense of reality. The narcissist is trying to monopolize their victim's sense of truth so that they are easier to abuse and to lead them into situations that they can exploit for benefit. This can easily cause depression, not to mention paranoia, and it can be a trigger. Many victims report a need to clarify every piece of information in conversation, no matter how unimportant. It's a life-ruining to experience because it takes away your own perspective on your life. It is an attempt to dehumanize you.

He says that you always hated the way his family looked. It makes you feel awful, he brings it up three, seven times a week. Every time he talks about it, your stomach drops lower.

Racking your brain, you try to summon up any sort of memory of the event. Gradually a moment comes back to you, from two seasons ago. You were getting ready to go to dinner. He was wearing the same color tie his father always wears.

You said he looked like his family, laughing about it. You forgot about it after that. He didn't. You thought it was nothing, but wounded pride does not abide. For the rest of your life, you will pay for that comment.

Already that was a year ago, but it's still around. So are so many other things, such as the fact that somehow you started every argument which ended in you crying. Apparently, you're too dramatic even though you can remember what he sounds like when he screams so well that you hear it a little while waiting in silence. You start to forget what you even said most of the time; it's not worth combing through life that meticulously.

Over the months, you grow quieter. You say less to your friends. In general, you're just sort of separated from life, floating through it. There's nothing you could imagine worth getting involved for. The risk is everywhere, who's to know what could get you yelled at. You stop calling your family, you stop going out with your friends, so much just falls away.

You don't want to defend yourself from anything or explain anything. You're too tired of living like everything is a debate. Love should be enough for you to look past what you disagree on.

That doesn't stop the hours every night that your words are raked over in front of you as he picks apart every moment of the day. Eventually, you grow numb to it and start agreeing to whatever he's saying, not even following his trains of thought anymore. You let his reality reign because you don't even want to be right; you just want to be comfortable again.

This leaves you isolated, with nothing to bounce off of. Everything you do has to be done through sheer force of will, turning your life into nothing but struggle and release. The best moments are the silent ones, where you get to watch the snow and forget about whatever is surrounding you.

That is because absence is becoming freer than being present in your life. That is a dire warning sign. Once you are freer in your life not contributing at all, then you've been left with no room for yourself. There is no stronger proof of being in an environment that does not value you.

As the years go on you become a shell of yourself, so faded in character and energy that you don't recognize yourself, much less who you wanted to become. Fear dominates everything so much to the point that you feel afraid to admit you are afraid. You cannot admit how much you are hurt for fear of being hurt worse. This is what it feels like to be trapped.

Narcissists require their victims to get to this point because it allows them to live their fantasies without interruption. Once you accept their lies as facts, then you are an extension of their delusion, so they can use you freely as fuel for their experience.

If you live like this, you will lose your mind. It is crucial for your self-trust and your independence that you form an image that stems from yourself first. This is difficult to do after living with a narcissist in your life, but it will bring a lot of presence and understanding back to you.

Once you can validate reality independently for yourself, you have defeated their influence over you. To do this, you need to take a step back and feel fully in your own feet, then judge for yourself. By having your own measure of reality you can identify the lies that the narcissist is injecting into your life.

Empaths are especially at risk when dealing with gaslighting. The instinct to believe is holy, it's how we got out of the caves, but it can also be a weakness if you do not know how to limit your trust. When you are not discerning enough, trust is gullibility.

That's why it's crucial to build up your own voice and input with the world. The most successful strategy is going to be to have your own way of bartering with your surroundings and getting away from believing the narcissist in your life. As you engage with them you are risking your mental stability, so there really is no good reason to. The best thing is going to be distance, and to get out of the abuse you must leave.

Find people who don't do this to you, people who let you have your own experience and perspective. Those people are healthy and will respect your contributions. Narcissists will not. There is no cure for their disorder. When you're around chemical weapons you do not clean the ground, you run.

Likewise, if a narcissist is gaslighting you, there is no better option than removing their opportunity to influence your life. You stand nothing to gain except for distrust for your own voice.

Empaths who are stuck in this situation should remember that at their core there is a social element. Once they can find their own voice independent from any influence, they should socialize with new people and experience different standards of how people treat each other. The isolation the narcissist encourages in the empath's life by stealing their energy is a threat to their mental health because it deadens the empath's gift.

To combat this they should, as everyone who has the influence of a narcissist in their life should, rediscover the natural balance between being alone and being around other people. Everyone will have a different experience with what harmony is, so there is no way to know what to do other than to listen to your own intuition and to pursue what from life appeals to you.

Humans are creatures motivated by interest. There exists in all of us that childlike sense for the world, a sort of primal taste. You have favorite times of the day, smells, and plants. All of those things matter to you. Preserve that importance and invest time in understanding it.

The more you have independence, the more protection you will have from the attempts to highjack your perspective. By independently verifying stories, information, and beliefs, you will be able to repair your own sense of reality.

Once it is strong enough, you shouldn't let it be talked over or corrected. Hold on to your truth privately even if arguing with them isn't worth it. Getting out is still the most important thing to do. Pursue life for yourself.

Law 3

«Protect Your Property; For Freedom is an Extension

of Ownership»

The Law of Commandeering

Above all, the narcissist is a person of taste. That's why they pick beautiful and giving people as their victims. They don't want to cause pain. They want to drain good hearted, harmless people. This is due to a complete lack of inner value in their life. When they take a moment to themselves, they are disgusted.

Because of this, they will groom their victims. They will study them. They stalk empaths for their interest, their sense of life. The narcissist always cringes back from true experience, so they long for the profound experience that HSPs have. If they cannot experience it themselves, then they will attempt to steal it.

Empaths are wired the opposite way. Instead of seeing life as advantages and resources, empaths see people as souls. They see life as a profound opportunity to gain experience. To them, life is lived in a state close to worship. They aim to appreciate the people around them and to share in their struggles.

This attitude serves empaths in many ways. In professional settings this allows them to obtain places that are in the center of their study, such as in the case of Plato, one of the founding voices of Western Philosophy.

Plato had many flaws, as all of us do, but one of his virtues was the understanding he had of the voices around him. The star of his philosophy wasn't himself, but a dear teacher of his that ended up executed by the state. He composed through inspiration from the world he saw around him and he tried to bring life to things outside of himself.

Through this project, we were given a platform to build off of that assumed polyphony over monologues. This is part of the richness of European philosophy because it has built within itself an understanding of perspective. There are different truths for different people. Empaths are especially aware of this and are capable of meeting others where they are speaking from, experiencing others' truths. Everyone can do this, and it's a healthy skill to practice, but empaths will find themselves engaging in it without thought.

With a lifestyle like this, the empath is regularly exposed to new opportunities to grow. If they take care of themselves then they end up being welcomed into the world and they find healthy places to inhabit. The narcissist does not have such options. By poisoning the world around them with selfishness, they have left themselves isolated.

To accommodate for this lack of positive interest in the world around them, the narcissists often target the natural goodwill that the empaths exude. They attach themselves to the empaths and take credit for the positivity in their life, trying to gain access to their interests and experience. Doing so is what they can manage to contribute to a healthy relationship with the world around them. Because of their condition, the closest narcissists can come to empathy is being a parasite.

Through being parasitic, they must be concerned with the health of their host. If they notice their target getting solemn or engaging less in the world they may worry about the quality of their supply.

Often they discard their victims when they become too depressed. The depression is usually triggered by the narcissists themselves, but they lack the awareness to understand that. Instead, they think the empaths are too weak and abandon them. Along with them, they bring a photographic memory of the empaths' interests and humor that they will use to charm their next victims. This is how they appropriate a personality to inhabit, using others' skin as a mask.

You were a painter in college. You love one painter for his utter freedom of form married to his classic understanding of composition, resulting in pieces as wild as another painter's, but more readable, more living. This has been thought of yours for years, but a piece of small talk for him. He spat it out while you were having coffee with acquaintances. You asked him if he had been looking into painting later that day, and he starts talking about how important one movement was for the modern art scene in general. You ask him how he got introduced to the school of art and he stares into your face, eyes dead, then answers, "You".

Of course, you knew that, and you knew that he knew that, but it was something else to get him to say it. He dodges admitting how much your influence has been a part of his life now. When you first started seeing him he was trying to inhale all of your interest without hiding it. He asked your opinions about art, about the geographical regions surrounding you, what drinks you liked, and what kind of music you were interested in. You talked to him like you would talk to anybody, with honesty.

He remembered everything you said. Now he plays your favorite music while he talks to clients at work. He brags about making deals over jazz which you introduced him to. All of your culture is thrown around his life at random like you're being blended.

In his habits and conversation, you see pieces of yourself float by, and your grip on who you are starts to get muddled. You forget why you were interested in what you were interested in because he's talked about it so many times it doesn't even sound like what you remember being interested in.

Your life has been turned into an aesthetic. Everything you used to be is now a hollow character that is paraded around you daily. He even took one of your mother's recipes. It takes you several minutes of conversational loops to get him to admit stealing something as little as that.

Everything that was taken you agreed to give, but it's the lack of appreciation that numbs you to who he is becoming. This isn't growing with you; it's growing from you, like something worse than being a mother.

Your own voice becomes strange to you because you don't know where it will end up. You're scared to say things because you don't want them to be repeated. The echo is maddening. The only place that you feel comfortable is in your head because he's always home.

This ends up making your voice untrained. You stop thinking in your native language and start thinking in pure intuition, a language that can't be dictated. The safest place for you is in utter abstraction, as that's somewhere he can't follow.

Living like this causes you to go gray. Your exercise schedule falls off. Your hobbies get less time, and food tastes like nothing. You shut off because of feeling so stolen from. There's less and less energy to devote to your life because it has been siphoned from you.

Essentially, you have been stolen from yourself and no longer have permission to be yourself. Empaths are especially in danger with this form of manipulation because they struggle with taking a stance for themselves. Narcissists thrive on control, so by dominating your sense of permission they feel free to steal from you as they like. This is one of the worst positions to be caught in.

The best-case scenario is that your significant other becomes a reincarnation of yourself in your worst years of childhood. The worst scenario is that they become a clone of you and then try to force you out of the very life you built for yourself. When someone who is intimate with you has this level of competition innate in them you will always be unsafe. Every moment is a fight. There is no pause from the conflict of interests.

What you need to do is learn how to keep private. You have talent, you have insight, and you have experience. Every life is worth something. Don't share this gift with people who won't appreciate it, find communities that will help you get further involved with what you already use as part of your definition of yourself.

To develop your relationship with yourself you must forgive yourself and let go of shame. Entertain your thoughts and instincts that are always present no matter the environment that you're in. These aren't fantasies; they're what you're actually interested in.

Be patient on this journey. Reestablishing a connection to your inner voice is a challenging task. Find your heart in silence, or what you remember when you're not thinking about anything. Our psyches will often hide our purpose in our peripherals. Realize that and then follow what motivates you.

If aesthetics have always called to you, then join the crystal community. Feel free to start being particular about your surroundings. Get more involved with how your mental state is affected by your environment. Go for walks in parks that you want to appreciate more. Cook meals that you're interested in learning. Invest in yourself the energy that you waste on someone who doesn't listen to you.

When you do this, you will teach yourself how to care about yourself first, and you will legitimize your own interest. This is a crucial part of identity because, no matter how empathic you are, you need to be able to decide things for yourself. Relying on other people's opinions is being codependent.

Empaths are prone to becoming codependent with narcissists because of the empaths' lack of a sense of self, and the narcissists' brazen sense of self. The empath might be trying to learn how to be strong from the narcissist, but all they will learn from this is how to be taken advantage of.

The empath is correct to want to know how to be independent, but the narcissist is an awful example. The empath needs to learn how to stand up for themselves, not how to cut other people out. Instead of learning from an unhealthy example, they need to feed their own sense of confidence and inner security.

Doing this may feel like being too self-centered to the empath, but it's very important to build a stronger and resilient personality. When the empath is able to set their own story and remember what they authentically care about, then they will not be prone to falling victim to manipulation that takes away their identity. They will know what feels wrong to them and when it feels like someone is pretending to be them. Once they can recognize those situations, they can learn to exit them.

It's paramount to identify the lies of the narcissist and keep them outside of your psyche. The way to reverse the damage is to do so, to reject everything they try to tell you, and everything they pretend to be. Remember who you are, what your positive qualities are, what your opinions are and stick to them.

Law 4

«An Undiagnosed Pain Will Always Be Misattributed

to Its Surroundings»

The Law of Equivalency

If you prick me, do I not bleed?
If I bleed, did you not prick me?
Don't wrestle with a pig,
You will get filthy, and it loves it.

The narcissist is obsessed with the game of power. At no point do they stop trying to game dynamics to find leverage over others. It is their entire life mission to dominate those around them. Part of their issue is solipsism, because they assume that everyone is working from the same perspective. Because of, they will gaslight others into taking part in their arguments, assuring them that they were involved in the first place.

This control of the narrative is so they can place everyone on the same level as themselves. Naturally, they're attracted to conflict and drama, as these are situations that can be exploited, but they never want that to be found out. If the world knew how sadistic they are they would face social stigma, so they make sure to frame everything from a point of view that displays them as well-meaning.

Since they need and want this perception of the situation, the narcissist will insist that they didn't start any argument, implying that disagreements were mutual. They will scream at you, but then bring up that you raised your voice too. Everything will be lost in this mutualism of responsibility that will cloud your intentions.

This misdirection is an important tool to the narcissist because it leaves the victim's mind working slowly, unsure of whether or not it is thinking clearly. Meanwhile, the narcissist is aware of his lies, so he's able to maneuver the situation with ease. Over time he has built a net around the victim and trapped them within their own doubt.

When the victim is lost it's easy for the narcissists to talk about whatever they want. One thing they look for from narcissistic supply is an audience, so while they have a confused person trapped by their charm they will use the opportunity to monologue and speak as they see fit. The victim will be lost in these conversations of unconnected abstract thoughts, but unable to speak up and question why the conversations are happening. This is because they're told that they are a part of them.

This dynamic appears often in relationships, but can also occur between a narcissistic parent and a child. It is an overstepping of your sense of time. Instead of listening to you and your interests, they create an image of you and expect you to play with along with them how they imagine you should. This is the unfortunate reality of being involved with a narcissist, they will never know you, they will only know the idea they have of you. You were never known as yourself to them, only what they judged you as.

Realizing this is often an incredibly painful experience to go through, as you like to believe that people who you share intimacy with respect you and your needs, but this is not always the case. Sometimes people come into your life who aren't interested in recognizing your independent voice. These are people who lack the social development to have meaningful relationships, and there really is nothing you can do other than to have sympathy for them.

Engaging with them is a dehumanizing experience. It is sacrificing your right to have your own opinions and voice. They will try to abuse your trust into convincing you that you want things that you don't really want. This risk is not worth the potential benefit of a relationship with them.

It's important to keep in mind that it isn't everybody who is coming with a healthy frame of mind. Many people are struggle with different things, and some people struggle with recognizing that other people have boundaries. These people are pitiable, but pity is one of the worst motivators for a human. It leaves you trying to act as a superior, and that's always an unflattering position.

You just want a day to go right. It's dinner with your parents, what could go wrong? It should be easy, a night out, even. The car ride is mostly him talking. You go numb and think about nothing. Then you're there, at the farm to table restaurant. You give your Mom and your Dad hugs, excited to see them.

The conversation is stilted. You laugh with your parents and talk about the family news with them, but your husband stays stiff, sulking over his plate. Like a child, he slouches at the table, looking past the conversation into other people's nights. His leg shakes under the table.

Trying to include him in the conversation, you bring up one of his achievements at work. Your mom says how impressed she is with it, but he just sniffles and brushes it off. You carry on with the conversation, talking about a trip you were planning in the spring.

Right then, he decides to talk about the abortion you had two months ago. The name of the child flashes through your mind. You feel sick, everything gets too hot. Your mother screams and puts her hands on you, asking if it's true. Your father looks at his hands. Your husband keeps talking, but by now you're crying so you rush to the bathroom.

By the time you exit, your parents left. Your husband remains, watching from the table. You can tell you're in for a long conversation, the way his posture sickly echoes that of a predator.

What did you do to deserve this? On the way back you find out. He couldn't believe you, that you had no respect for his social anxiety. Your parents always stressed him out, how could you forget that? And then you just ran off, leaving him with them. How could you?

How could you, after you offered him the invitation, telling him it was okay to say no? How could you, after you've spent months coaching him through conversations and how to relax? How could you, after he convinced you that now wasn't the time for a child?

You asked him how it was fair for him to bring up information like that to your parents. He blew up and asked how it was fair to parade him around like a show pony. You wiped away tears then apologized, saying that was never your intention. He said it was okay. You said you were still upset. He went back to screaming. You started crying again.

Conversations like this were the rule, not the exception. You were always arguing and somehow it was an argument when you were always just being yelled at. A few times you raised your voice back at him, at the beginning of the cycle, but it got you nowhere, you just felt guilty.

Over time you grew to accept that, no matter what you did, you would be seen as a combatant, so you agreed with him that you were at odds, that you were arguing about everything. Once everything you said stopped being listened to, or it was appropriated to mean something else, there was no reason to speak.

Even down to your little pieces of advice, like that he should learn to type from the home row for his desk job, anything that could be perceived as an insult was. Your own intention got lost in translation because he was never listening to you. He was using you to act out the dramas inside his head.

This behavior wears at the conditioning of the soul. It trains the body to always expect conflict, to be lost in stress, and to dread every conversation. You should not have to prove everything you say. An insistence on clarity is often a symptom of recovery from narcissistic abuse.

For empaths, it retrains their instinct, one of community, into one of withdrawal. It constantly leaves them tired and untrusting, which is death for someone who lives through their connection to other people.

The entirety of the narcissist's perspective is unhealthy. When you internalize that, through empathizing with them, you are internalizing negative energy that may cause major damage to your psychic health. There is no healthy influence they can have on you, because all of their thoughts are centered on the position that they matter more than everybody else. That position is unfixable. When someone adopts it, they're toxic.

Relief from this environment can return the color of your life. To experience such relief, it is as simple as asserting the boundaries that you know your narcissists will not respect.

If he does not get along with your family, do not invite him to them. If he hits your dog because it's too needy, don't let him look after it. Essentially, remove all vulnerability that you can. Prevention is one of the greatest tools against narcissistic abuse. Once you give them trust there's no telling how much muck they will shove into your psyche.

Also, extend into the healthier parts of your life. Develop new relationships in a town with new standards. Find places where you feel respected and like you can speak up for yourself. Doing so may require some inner work on your part, but doing so will benefit you.

Remember to be the friend for yourself that you want to be for others.

By finding experience separate from the narcissist, you will become less clouded by their influence. You will also be less held down by the perceptions that they try to force into your mind. It is always possible to retrain yourself and to find your way back into the world, no matter how much the narcissist tries to make you afraid of it or discourages you from doing so.

Putting yourself first is one of the most powerful strategies when working to get away from narcissistic abuse because it targets their supply at the root. They can take advantage of you by taking the energy you should use for self-care and monopolizing it themselves. When you are able to redirect this energy to where it belongs, to yourself, you will be effectively cutting them off from the supply, and taking back your access to your resources.

Self-love will always be a potent cure to most psychological difficulties, whether they are chemical or environmental. By being patient with ourselves, and by being good friends to ourselves, we encourage our body to feel comfortable being itself, and we calm down. There are few better ways to handle stress than by being patient with ourselves. We must know that we will handle what we can, and that will be adequate.

Perfection is the aim of the narcissist. They insist on the quality of things and are obsessed with judgment. This is an unhealthy paradigm to pick up, and so the more you can distance yourself from that obsession, and the more you can be at peace with the chaotic nature of the universe, the more stable you will be.

Law 5

«You Will Always Be Responsible If You Choose to Take Part»

The Law of Duty

A Victim's Rights.

Like a prince, the narcissist expects the world to be ordered. Naturally, the order that perceives revolves around him. There are the insignificant that can be brushed off, forgotten about because they can't comprehend the divine gift that his presence represents - then there are the chosen, those that can see how special he is, how important his life will be.

For these people he sees a natural duty falling onto them, one that is to flatter his weaknesses and speak to his strengths. A great man is not made alone. It takes draining a village, especially women.

Narcissists love to play the victim because of how much it allows them to access. By engaging with the pity of other people they can find money, places to stay, opportunity, and more. They know how to manipulate social situations too, so they become excellent at engaging with pity while avoiding looking like a beggar.

They expect the people around them to play along with this perception, that the narcissist is always an underdog, with the world weighing down on them. Often, they will want this to be reflected in flattery, getting compliments by raising the bare minimum amount of effort they put in. Never do the stories that they tell about themselves line up, but the price to pay for contradicting them is dear.

While at odds, the narcissists will always insist on your guilt. If you are intimate with them, they will carry this expectation almost inherently, as if they are too mature to have a negative influence on others. They pretend to be great, so they can't be a villain, so they will never admit to villainous actions.

Even if they start the argument, you will be at fault. There is no way to avoid this tactic because the narcissist has assumed your guilt before they started talking, that's the tactic. There's no way for you to communicate with them for them to change their mind, they've already passed judgment over your case.

This allows them to always assume the stronger bartering position because at the heart of the narcissist is an eye for an eye, a tooth for a tooth. They see any sort of pain, perceived or otherwise, to be the perfect justification for making demands over others.

It is important to note here, too, that the narcissist is not engaging in conversation at this point, they are engaging in manipulation. The social interaction is not done to understand another person, but to take something from their target. They don't want relationships, they want resources.

So be wary of being in this situation. If you internalize the guilt it will never stop coming, and you will be made to feel terrible when you've done nothing wrong. This is a dangerous position to be caught in, for it can launch you into the worst depression of your life.

The narcissist will try to convince you that you are someone you've never been, cruel, manipulative, and uncaring. This is not who you are, but a mean-spirited caricature. If you listen it will make you feel awful because someone is lying about who you are. The guilt is not real; it is being forced upon you. You did nothing wrong, and it is okay to be you. Life does not need to be conflict.

If you find yourself in this situation, keep in mind that you have a right to perception too, and everything isn't how it is told to you. You shouldn't believe everything someone else says, you can make your own judgments. If you feel like you did nothing wrong, chances are you didn't.

How could you forget that asking him to take care of laundry this week would be a trigger? How dare you listen to late night television when his father used to? Did you forget about him? Does he not matter to you anymore?

More and more dramatic conversations are triggered by simple things you said, attempts to communicate with each other as lovers do. Yet, again and again, simple things you want to express or share are spiraled out into stressful episodes.

Slowly, over the months, everything has fallen into this domain of triggers and issues. There is nowhere you can express, nothing you can enjoy, without upsetting him. He has to be the master of things, he's the interesting one. He's the one that knows.

You feel like there's no space for you to be, like everything you do is an encroachment. Everything you say is a criticism to him, every opinion you have is a personal attack. If you mention an actor, you will be kept up for three days while he rants about how unfair the standards for men are. There is nothing for you to enjoy without crisis or being made to feel like a villain for doing so.

For hours you listen to him talk about interest after interest, hero after hero. Nights of your life have been drained this way, and there's no progress. Maybe he started a project, maybe he succeeded at something, but you've been forgotten. There's no room for anything anymore, it either hurts him or is distracting.

Meanwhile, he fills every spare space that he can find. His interests litter your apartment, with CDs and magazines strewn along several surfaces. He will speak to you in depth for hours about what drummer he thinks deserve the title of the best drummer of the 80s, but he has no concern about the concerts that are coming up. One of those shows you've had your eyes on for months.

In this environment, you're going to end up walking on eggshells. That's the only way to cope with such an anal way of going about life. You can never drop your poise, for the criticism will be immediate, and the damage you will be said to have caused will be so dramatic that it's better for you to omit everything. This is like living under military occupation.

When caught in this dynamic, your voice will be manipulated into something different from your nature. That is a very damaging scenario as it severs your connection with your inner voice. It is important to realize how you're talking and how much of it is a reaction. Try to isolate your response and realize how the narcissist is making you act.

If you are holding back opinions or engagement because of these reactions, be wary of that. It is a symptom of someone stealing the energy that you need to live. Make sure to be aware of those sensations and follow them to their root, there is something that you need to address.

Once somebody loses their voice, they lose their ability to communicate with the world outside of themselves. This is a drastic situation because it limits their ability to participate and to receive assistance. Without the ability to reach others, the victim becomes at risk of having to depend on the narcissist.

Dependence is what the narcissist uses to retain their victims over time. Because they can't contribute meaningfully or fairly, they manipulate their way into the lives of others through reliance.

Let this be your life, and you will lose all interest in everything. He will box you out from the world around you. It's a modern form of enslavement, basically mining for feelings. To combat the hollowness in his own chest he has decided to target your warmth, to steal it. Labeling himself a victim, he will become your tyrant.

The best thing to do is to refuse these duties. If you must perform to retain living circumstances, support him as much as you would support yourself, but no more. Don't read endless books you don't care about, don't listen to his music that he won't even release publicly. Don't be a resource, be a person. Make him respect your interest. Make him admit that you exist, too.

Whether you are a child, friend or lover, you should never be merely an audience member in somebody else's life. If someone tries to force this dynamic on you, they have an obvious sense of disrespect for the world outside of themselves.

When engaged with other people, make sure you are participating too. Everyone gets something out of being social, so make sure that you get what you need. Unfortunately, things aren't fair in the world, and sometimes you must take to receive.

Realize what is worth standing up for, and don't fall too far into being argumentative. That is exactly the game they play, and if you walk away with it, then they have taught you it. The most effective cure for abuse is forgiving and letting go of the experience, not fighting to beat it.

Represent what you actually believe deserves representation. Fill your life with the opportunity to be an agent for the changes that you want to see in the world. The atmosphere is contributed by everyone, so go out and be a part of the world. Don't let the narcissist corner you and make you forget how much is out there.

Positive affirmation is one of the most powerful tools in our psychology. Our psyche is built to react to it incredibly well. If you can handle the risks from gaining new associations with patience, it will be rewarded.

At first branching out can be awkward, especially after being hounded by narcissistic abuse, but eventually it will start to feel natural again. The more times it goes well, the more you will have faith that there is a world out there for you to access.

Energy is one of the dominant factors in this process. To truly get better and heal, you must attract positivity, which means letting go of the fight within yourself. This is a difficult process and may not be attained all at once, but the more you can relax into a positive relationship with the world, the more blessings will come to you.

Empaths stand to lose a lot from guilt manipulation because they internalize other peoples' opinions so readily. By being so believing they are immediately at risk of a narcissist manipulating them. This trust is attractive to narcissists because it means the empath is easy to program.

Most of the empaths are quickly convinced that they are the problem. By naturally seeking harmony, they are prone to react to negative energy and to attempt to solve it by changing themselves. This flexibility is crucial for their ability to get along with others, but it's not a shapeshifting ability.

Empaths still have a natural personality and set of boundaries. Just because they are so willing and able to accommodate other people does not mean that they can act like doormats. The appropriate use of this gift is to be able to interact with all different sorts of people for short periods of time, not to be caught inside with someone who wants to privatize.

Law 6

«You Must Always Listen While Not Being Listened

to»

The Law of Conversation

Me first, then Me again.

The empathic approach to conversation is a passive one. It is based on a give and take, an expression and a return. Most empaths are not trained to recognize a pretender. Because of this, the narcissist can become adept at mimicking this form of conversation while not partaking in it.

This is easy to see when the inauthenticity of narcissists is remembered. They don't feel bad about manipulating or lying in social environments to get what they want. One of their most lusted for prizes is attention, and so if one just has to pretend to listen for it, they're making a good deal. All they have to do is nod and repeat back enough of the conversation to pretend that they care.

By doing this narcissists are able to turn their target into a supply of attention, using them to process their thoughts. Doing so is how they figure out how to relate to other people. Because of their lifestyle, they end up separated from the rest of the world and unaware of how to properly associate with it. They are aware of this, but not aware of how to work on the issue, so they clothe their ideas in the flesh of those around them.

The only way that they can be charming is through examining people and how they react to stimuli. They don't engage with the heart or with honesty, they always have a goal. Empaths are perfect targets for the narcissist because they are so in tune with the world around them.

Essentially, the empath is worth several sources of supply because the empath provides insights into several different sorts of people. Because of their sensitivity to the world, they naturally grow a deep understanding of other people. The narcissist can take advantage of this by picking apart the empath's understanding. This allows the narcissist to gain access to knowledge that's hard to come by while only having to expose himself to one person.

Interactions with the narcissist will leave the empath confused. The empath finds balance in life through interactions with others, so when they are analyzed, but not listened to, by the narcissist the empath will grow numb. Empaths often learn who they are through their interactions, so when interactions are perpetually cold and one-sided the empath will feel out of place.

The empath will meet difficulty trying to break free from this dynamic because the narcissist will be very insistent that nothing is wrong. Because of their giving nature, it will take some time for the empath to realize something is out of balance, but the narcissist is taking without giving. This is unsustainable in relationships because eventually, the empath will run out of resources to share.

Figuring out how to remove themselves from the narcissist's influence will be another challenge. Empaths are naturally welcoming people, which means it's harder for them to set boundaries and turn people away. To move forward in life, and especially in situations involving narcissists, they need to learn how to say no and stand by it.

Setting boundaries with narcissists is the only way to protect against their advances. When they demand time, there is nothing to do but box them out. Once they are given anything they will expect more. Starve their source of supply and they will usually move on to more promising opportunities.

If these boundaries are not enforced then the narcissist will continue to prey on the victim. They don't take no, they must be shown no through commitment and physical means. By making yourself not available, you will communicate to them that they have to put in an effort to associate with you that they're not willing to.

At first, he remembered so much about you. He picked up tulips after your first date. Then you had told him about that time at summer camp you got to watch the greenhouse. At graduation, he picked you up from school and you went out drinking. He remembered your favorite bars that you went to over the years. He remembered your siblings' names, that you used to play soccer, and that your favorite fruit is pineapple.

So what happened? Now he doesn't even remember your job, the way you like your coffee or your anniversary. It's like sleeping with a stranger. The first nights were like sleeping with a husband. Were you catfished? After the marriage, it was just a different person, someone who would accept you doing all of the chores, but not that you liked sleeping on the right side of the bed.

Yet all these little rules have been a part of your life for so long that you've grown accustomed to them. You know not to close cabinets too loud in the morning, and that sugar is served next to the coffee, not in it. You've stopped listening to several of your favorite bands because he said they were too noisy and triggered his headaches.

Everything that was a part of you has become a complaint. Before it was great how interested you were in the arts, now you're a dreamer. At first, he loved that you were always trying to do something, now you're too impulsive.

You get no say in his actions, though. Nothing that he does can annoy you because apparently everything he does is normal. It's the standard. You're the one who is misbehaving and making things not work out when they don't.

The dishes are how the dishes have to be, according to his explanation. He lacks the energy. He needs to watch the same news stories over and over because he needs to be up to date, yet he refuses to give up the TV for thirty minutes for you to watch a show as you cook dinner.

There are endless excuses from him, while you are left with no space to exhibit your natural tendencies. You try to express it, but there are no words that you feel you can use without him complaining about how you're talking to him. The idea of holding him accountable at all scares you because of how much drama it will cause.

Over time, you grew to expect to say nothing during the conversations you have other than to express approval of what he has said. It was the only way to get through the day without being shamed for being cruel. All you had to say in your own home was that you agreed with what was being said, or that you were impressed by it.

This led you to feel trapped and confused. How did someone who cared about you so much before end up leading such a hollow life, a rejection of what makes life beautiful? Before you felt empowered by his attention because it was applied lavishly to the most insignificant parts of you, but now even your core is left cold as he obsesses over whatever else has his attention.

You were tricked into thinking that he cared about you. This is hard to realize because you let him have a legitimate place in your life, but that is how manipulation works. Once he can convince you that he cares about you as much as you care about him, he withdraws from his contributions to the relationship while continuing to use it as a resource.

Narcissists are often difficult to perceive as liars because of their excellent memory. While they are selecting you as a target, they store information about your occupation, your interests, your dreams, and anything meaningful to you. They will then invest in these subjects, giving nuanced compliments and showering special attention on you. This is a tactic to earn your trust and assure you they're listening and invested in your life.

The reason they do this is that they have a childish interpretation of what attention is. Instead of recognizing listening as an active activity, they perceive it as certain ways of phrasing information or showing interest in others. They don't understand the natural flow of conversation and growing to trust another person, so they imitate it by memorizing things and pretending to be moved by them.

Over time even this false effort becomes tiring for them. Upkeep of their mask will slow down and they will know less and less about you, occasionally falling back on things they learned in the beginning.

During this period it becomes much easier to identify that they're not treating you like a person because they will not have reacted to anything going on in your life.

The narcissist struggles to see that life changes over time, to see that people expand and grow. Most of them suffer from some sort of arrested development. With this comes an underdeveloped sense of judging other people. Instead of getting to know somebody overtime, they rely on a high school cafeteria sense of judgment.

If you live believing their perspective, internalizing this immature way of processing the world, then you will internalize their stunted development. The world will become shallower as you engage with it in more basic ways, like considering whether or not things are good according to the standards of the narcissist.

Under these circumstances, the heart either grows to expect abuse as normal, or it becomes paranoid. You either let yourself become an emotional prostitute or withdraw from everything. There are ways to justify it, such as the sensitivities of the narcissist, or how intelligent they are, but that's nonsense. No one deserves to talk over you. When someone does so they are negating your right to communicate, to express yourself independently. Getting in the way of that right is to make it so that someone is isolated from the rest of us.

That isn't how you deserve to feel as a human. We are at our best when we can trust one another and feel a part of something larger. This species is a social species, and your health relies on your perception of several different relationships in your life. If you do not tend to your needs as a social animal, then you are neglecting your needs in general.

To undo the damage, you have to return to yourself. Explore passions and interests that were an important part of your life before you were exposed to narcissistic energy. The part of you that wants to be you is always intact; there are just layers of tar to peel back before it's exposed. It's difficult to do so but have faith. You can always love yourself again.

Find your voice through the things that feel like they're yours. You have music that was important to you once, try to rediscover it. Go to a new museum and listen to a guide. Do anything to kick start your interest in participating with the world. When you do this, you will be training your brain that your time is meant to be invested in bettering your life, not commiserating with somebody who doesn't want to get better.

Law 7

«There is No Neutral on the Field of Battle»

The Law of Heresy

With me or against me.

Narcissists dramatize life into something that even theatre can't recreate. Every moment, every conversation, every person, and every setting is something that can be played to their advantage. Because of this, they often run into conflict while trying to complete their control.

The games of manipulation they play never end, thus they rely on everything they can manipulate to be involved in their plans. There is no not getting involved in their drama. Once they trust you because you will become instrumental in their plots for gaining resources and influence.

They will use you for such leverage without thought because they don't think it's an odd thing to do. Naturally, humans use association as a way of spreading trust because they trust their friends and families to make good connections with the people around them. The narcissist can perceive this, but can't process the feeling of trust that the rest of us do.

Because of this, they create another imitative device. By using you, and whoever else they can influence, they create an image of being trustworthy because they associate with trustworthy people, such as yourself.

While the target of this strategy, the victim will be put in many awkward situations. The narcissist will expect them to support their lies and manipulation, so the victim will be pressured to lie in association with them. Should the narcissist become too obvious with their manipulation, or be discovered, then the victim risks being seen as complicit in the actions of the narcissist. This stress is another tool that the narcissist implements to test loyalty. By putting you through such high-risk situations they are reaffirming your commitment to them.

Your reputation will most likely suffer from being involved with them. Even if you are able to displace their manipulation and prevent yourself from manifesting it, people will still be able to see something is wrong with you. It will be obvious from how tired you are and how hesitant to interact with others you are that someone has been draining your energy. Most people don't know to read this as a sign of narcissistic abuse, so it will be difficult to receive the help you need if you don't communicate efficiently. If you don't, most people will think that you've stopped taking care of yourself, not that you've been abused.

If you live with this influence for long enough, you will develop a legitimate case of PTSD. Once you're trained to be so high strung, when everything is watched and criticized, it's hard to forget that standard. The conversation will be processed as battles by you as you think about the advantage someone may be trying to gain over you.

This will produce difficulties with getting out of the situation. What you need to do is to feel comfortable trusting the people around you, but when you're around a narcissist that is one of the most dangerous things to do. Instead, be aware of how you're feeling, that will be the way to figure out how to heal.

If you feel well enough to return back to society and hang out with your friends again, embracing the casual setting, then do that. If you feel you need to become defensive until you can find enough space away from the narcissist to express, that is also legitimate. Respect how you are feeling and take care to find what good feels like to you. Take care of yourself and nurture yourself. You were neglected and need to repair from the situation, it's okay to be tender.

So, however, you are comfortable doing so, tend to your own needs and you will be able to wrestle free from this influence. If you don't then you will lose more opportunities than you will be aware of. Having a narcissist in your life is like having a power plant of negative energy. That will extend into your aura.

You find yourself in an awkward position. You boyfriend has lied in front of your coworkers to look more impressive. He said that he was a contractor, but his only experience was remodeling your basement. He ruined the tile then left it unfinished. Still, he looks to you for support, smiling to you as he lies. You confirm his story with a nod, wishing there was something strong to sip.

Because of this conversation, one of your coworkers hires him to work on their garage. Your boyfriend takes on the job, accepting a $200 advance. Months later the work still isn't done and your boyfriend refuses to talk to your coworker. Instead, you have to play the middleman, explaining that projects take time and that she just needs to wait for a while.

Eventually, your coworker goes to small claims court. The relationship between you two is ruined. Your boyfriend paints it as not a big deal and suggests that you move on. He says that he did nothing wrong and that things will work out in court. He ends up getting fined.

After this work is just one of the most awkward experiences of your life. Your coworker talked to the rest of the office, and you can't really argue against what she said. Instead, you have to swallow your shame as eyes follow you, thinking thoughts that you don't want to imagine.

Over the course of your relationship, the lies have become expected from you. At gas stations and at parties you're expected to keep up with backstories and characters that he builds. At first, it felt like living a second life, a childhood prank over the rest of the world, but then it grew to feel like a weight that you carried with you everywhere. You feared making friends, knowing it would only be a matter of time before he targeted them.

You get treated like a selfish person by the people around you because of your association with him. They start to think that you're in on it, that you want to take the advantages that he does. You don't stop him, so it's hard to defend yourself. Instead, you grow quieter.

This finalized the decay of your social relationships, and the workplace that used to feel so familiar now feels like somewhere you're trespassing. It's harder and harder to be a part of the things because any situation can be taken from. You're afraid to expose people to your relationship like you're diseased.

Shame like this will ruin your experience of life. From disease to malaise, being treated like this demotivates your body. As the relationship goes on it will be harder for you to convince yourself to summon the energy required to take care of yourself.

He treats you like an accomplice, too, which makes you wonder if you are. The way he talks about the manipulation in front of you is so blatant. If you had a problem with it, wouldn't you speak up?

If you felt comfortable, you would. The way the narcissist manipulates intimacy is that they condition you to be afraid of expressing yourself. By continually providing negative stimuli in reaction to your expression, they are training you into accepting the things around you without question.

They don't want to go through the effort of convincing you things are worth doing, they just want you to do them, this is why they condition you to be terrified of talking back.

Letting yourself be taken over like this is the equivalent of being objectified. The body gets better at whatever it does, that's how neural pathways are strengthened, so when you are used as leverage in conversation your body remembers that. It will leave you used to being lived through, of being run by a parasite.

The best thing to do is to disengage it. You will run the risk of confrontation when you call them out for lying, but there is always the option to omit. Let them dig their own graves and don't contribute when they expect you to. Stop being a part of their unit and start being independent. If they want to be in your life, they have to let you have your life.

If you are able to separate the narcissist from how you are perceived, then you will be able to bargain with the world for yourself. Freed of their influence it will be much easier for you to form healthy associations, as you will not be weighed down by their negativity or manipulation. This is a healthy association because you are presenting your own energy and living with respect for it, rather than acting as a tool for the narcissist to gain advantage over your surroundings.

Once you act in your own interest and are honest, people will remember you for who you are. Naturally, people want people to remember, so this is no surprise. We are creatures that depend on the social experience for our wellbeing mentally, economically, and in all other forms. Engage with this and build up your social instinct, your social currency. When you invest time and energy in the world around you, it builds a memory of you. It has a reason to be invested in who you are and how you're doing.

The more you receive positive affirmation from people the more confident you will feel in yourself. When other people appreciate you and respect your boundaries then you settle into that as the new norm. This retraining process is the best way to address the issues the narcissist left you with because it reintroduces you to healthy social standards. After being surrounded by narcissists' energy we tend to internalize that and forget that we deserve better, that there's more to life for us then bickering and plotting.

As you do this, the narcissist will be upset. They hate to lose more than anything, and losing one of the parts that manipulated for advantage hits home. It's difficult for them to respect your personal sovereignty, so they won't see this as you trying to set boundaries. They will see it as a betrayal.

There is no way to work against this interpretation. Like a person suffering from paranoia, they will have their own understanding of the circumstance and refuse to react to outside information. Convincing them that you just want space or what's best for both of you won't be possible. They're not going to listen to you. They're going to continue manipulating.

With this in mind, it is best to heal as you can. Preserve that healing through keeping it separate from the narcissist. Do not try to share your exploration into the world with them, they will either devalue it or try to appropriate it.

Instead, heal for yourself, by yourself. Define your life by your own standards and experiences independently. If you get too close to the narcissist they will use you for bargaining or something of that sort, so don't. You may love them, but it's better to have a decent life than to be tortured by people that may not even love you as you love them.

Law 8

«You Will Bend, Then Bend Further»

Zeus' Law

Obedience does not make a good wife, but a good wife is obedient.

Everyone has a right to say no. Your body is yours, your life is yours. There's no reason to be persuaded that anyone else has a right to your habits, actions, or beliefs. A narcissist does not see this and finds areas to encroach on everywhere.

Their persona of ruler allows them unlimited rights to all things, including you. They perceive themselves as a superior being, hence this gives them the right to lord over your life. Through criticism and through command, they will police your habits into a routine out of their imagination.

They do this so that they can be worshiped by someone. Everybody needs influences, but no one needs the influence that the narcissist has to offer. After convincing you that they're trustworthy, they will use their influence to design you. Influence is supposed to be like a suggestion, a light push from a friend to encourage you on your journey. With the narcissists that push feels more like bindings that they wrap around you, making sure that you tremble to think differently than how they want you too.

After they brand you with their touch, they will expect you to retain the form they left you in. If you don't, they take it is a personal affront. This dynamic betrays a codependent relationship.

By working around the natural tendencies for self-doubt and insecurity, narcissists are able to attach themselves to that process by representing the opposite. They target your inability to be brazen and show you the strength that they're willing to share with you if you let them speak for you. This can be very attractive to people with low amounts of self-trust.

The dynamic that they want to create is that of the king or the father. They want the paternal rights of an imaginary feudalistic era, to be able to tend to their homes without question or conversation, although women managed the household throughout history. In their idealistic fantasy, they see themselves as breadwinner and beloved, doing a little work to great effect, and being adored as a hero. Perhaps this lifestyle would be fine, but after they achieved enough to deserve it.

Instead, they will try to implement this fantasy into their lifestyle at the cost of you. To feel godly, they will make you into a servant, someone who listens to their decrees and critiques, who lives in accordance with their image. It'll take a while for them to do so, too slow for you notice unless you're looking for it.

Once you do notice it, it will be disgusting. The risks that come from having this energy in yourself is to become an entirely different person than you want. They will have had influence over your friends, your hobbies, your habits, and everything else that you can imagine. Over time, they creep into all corners of your mind, leaving nothing sacred.

Despite how great they may seem to you, don't let them change the way you hold your face. No one gets to say how others should look. Remember that there are no living gods, only people. You get as much respect as anyone else does, there are no kings. We've gotten past that. There is no rule for you to follow other than what makes you feel like living. Never lose sight of what is meaningful to you or else you will not guard your time. When life is not holy it is not protected. You deserve care and respect. Give yourself it if you cannot find it in the world.

Your personality may atrophy under the rule of a narcissist. This is concerning, but it is not something you can't heal from. Have patience and faith, you will be able to rebuild the things that you lost.

Over the years, your legs have been trained out of their muscle memory. All through your teens you drove with a foot on the window during long trips, but that's not proper, according to him. It's dangerous, completely irresponsible. So you don't do that anymore.

How many other little things were lost? Can you remember how you used to hold yourself before you crumpled in to hide all of your features? Or was it all lost under little comments, grudges that you didn't want to see the end of? The list of what's wrong with you grows every year. There's more and more to conceal.

You can see so much more life in your face in pictures from even two years ago. Your smile is a bit more awkward, but it's honest. Your eyes light up with energy like you could just jump out and be yourself at any moment. The person that you see is someone that you were proud to be, but you can't find her anymore.

Instead, you see a lack of color. Your hair has been falling out and this dead glaze has become permanent over your eyes, like oil. He's made it so that you know what it feels like to scream in public. By wearing at you every day with how you shouldn't act, you got to a point where you had the end of it. You've never screamed at anybody else, but you've screamed at him in a restaurant when he told you how to hold your fork. It was no reason to raise your voice, but you had to. He had been picking at you all day.

If it wasn't your hair making you look like a slut, then it was your opinions being too underdeveloped. You didn't have enough understanding. You didn't take proper care of yourself, whatever he wanted to make up. The only way to get along was to be quiet and agree with his attitude, but you're an adult too. There's no reason that someone should be able to hold you in a corner.

So you fought back and the restaurant stared at you. Someone started recording on their cellphone. You didn't know how to react so you just got the food put in a box and left, waiting in the car. He finished the meal and had a few drinks, then made you drive home. The night was remembered by him as one of your days, a scene that was caused by your unpredictable moods.

Never has he admitted that there's something weird about continually pressing into somebody else's psyche. When you bring it up to him, he dismisses it and you feel like a child. There's no place for your side, only words to obey. If you don't, then expect him to make you pay.

Entire nights can be spent with you being yelled at by the bedside even though you have work in the morning, but that's never brought up. What's brought up is the restaurant scene because he considers it humiliating. Like it wasn't humiliating to show up to work with baggy eyes and a headache? Like that didn't show everyone in the office exactly what you were going through? Like his abuse is something that you should be proud of?

The balance will never be even because the dynamic is not between equals. He has turned you into his subject and expects the respect due to an idol. This will take the life out of you because he will use all of it that he can. Narcissists need supply because they can't create positivity for themselves, so they thrive off others treating them like gods. That's the closest thing they can feel to having an authentic self-image, by warping somebody else's perspective of them.

This is foot binding for the soul. The human adult is not like clay, it will not take whatever form you press it into. It is firm and has its own shape, attributes, and character. Reforming it only does a disservice to the original, and so a narcissist's attempt to police your being can never improve you, it can only try to keep your soul in a glass cage or mangle it into an unrecognizable shape.

Despite how charming they may be, or how competent they may present themselves as, there is no valid reason to sacrifice your own control over your life to anyone. Whenever you are codependent on somebody, that means you require them to process life. This means you can't do it yourself, no matter what, you are always in need of something outside yourself. This is a disadvantage. It's stunting yourself by requiring external factors for you to grow.

To reverse it follow the shame that the narcissist has left you with. Follow all the shame you have and see how much of it stems from their actions, then commit to all of the things they tried to turn you against. Learn how to do what they made you afraid to do. Learn how to take your own risks and make your own environment. By going against their rules you will be recommitting to yourself rather than allowing them to have undue influence.

With parents, this relationship is especially difficult considering the authority they had or have over your life. They may use that as leverage to convince you that they are a better leader for your life than you could be, but that is abusive behavior. Elders have experience for us to learn from, but no healthy elder thinks they know what the youth should do with their lives.

Everybody is born into chaos. Life is something that we must all react to and contribute to on the terms that we see fit. No one will ever figure that out correctly, or forever. Humans will forever be born and be faced with that challenge. It is our right and responsibility to struggle with that. Infants must trust others to do that for them, but as soon as you can take care of yourself, then this journey is your journey. It might be scary, but facing your fears is one of the ways that we grow as people.

So take your right to state what this world is like. Stand up for yourself and apply your voice to the world around you. Practice creating your own opinions and standards. Often you will overshoot and act a little mean, but that is honestly something we all must go through when learning to speak. How are you supposed to defend yourself if you don't know how to hurt other people?

Keep that in mind as you learn, though. The point is not to learn how to become mean, but how to stand up for yourself with conviction. By strengthening your voice, you will become able to hold those that want to silence you at bay.

Once you inhabit yourself, you become much harder to manipulate because there is something solid behind you. By building your own confidence, you will naturally become unattractive to manipulative people because it will take too much effort to sucker you.

Ultimately many people, and many empaths, enjoy having a friendly and trustworthy appearance. This is completely understandable and you shouldn't change yourself because of other people, but you can still learn what it is to be firm. The greatest swordsmen feel no pressure to use their weapons. All the same, they are familiar with technique.

Law 9

«A Spouse has Certain Rights»

Hera's Law

Marriage has responsibilities, and I have needs.

In our society we have roles, and with those roles come expectations that are supposed to be fulfilled. There is the respect you should give your mother, the respect you should give your teacher, and the respect you should give bus drivers. Everyone deserves our appreciation and has a certain right to receive attention from us, even if it is a simple 'thank you'. The narcissist is aware of this, and if they become a spouse, they are certain to never let you forget it.

For them a wedding contract is not the happiest document in your lives, it's a signed agreement for you to be their supply. They will use the legal bonds that you danced into to restrain you and convince you that you have responsibilities to them. If you're their wife, then you must cook. If you're their husband, then your money isn't only yours. They will use marriage to blur boundaries.

They do this because it's an easy way of concealing their interest. Instead of looking like outright manipulation, they can hide behind social norms. They're not acting weird. They're acting as a spouse does. They're just living as normal people do. You're the one out of place. This is what they want to convince you of. By maintaining this dynamic, they can extract whatever they want out of you while hiding behind the tradition.

This trains the voice out of you because they bring legal and societal backing to their demands. Everything is normalized by them as your responsibility, so your labor and energy are extracted from you without remorse. As it goes on, they will leave you drained. This too will be explained away as the normal woes of the condition you are in, not given credence as exhaustion.

Once given enough time, they will manipulate around you. Through the intimate connection they have to you they will have access to your friends and family. Before you can spread information among your own people, they will have made a different version available. Your options will be to go along with it or try to correct what was said, which means changing how everybody already thinks.

Because of the trust you gave them in your life, they will have incredible access to the resources in your life and your lines of communication. Trying to reverse engineer their efforts will prove frustrating, if not impossible.

If they are talented enough with their evil arts, then they will be able to turn your support networks against you. The best way to react is to prevent them from being able to do so by establishing strong boundaries, but after it happens often you may need to form new social networks that they don't have access to. This is unfortunate, but better than being coated in the negativity the narcissist has spread throughout your life.

Otherwise, you will question whether or not you're a liar. Those close to you will be so influenced by the opinions of the narcissist that you will hear the narcissist's lies from so many mouths that you may begin to believe them. It's hard to keep everything in mind when the narcissist has a group of people to manipulate because then it's impossible to track which lie is coming from where. Tracing back the genealogy of every lie is also a much more tiring endeavor than it is to spread lies. That is why fighting with a narcissist is so inadvisable, they don't fight fair. You won't be fighting with a person. You will be wrestling with a spider.

Regardless of who you are, getting married to a narcissist is a dangerous endeavor. Once they have legally trapped you, they will feel much more comfortable pressing past your boundaries and convincing you to become what they want you to be.

Their goal in doing so is to establish rights and expectations on you through as little work as possible. By hiding behind a marriage contract, they are able to extract labor and attention from you without having to admit that they're draining you. The social tradition of the union is nothing more than an opportunity to put you in a position where they can take advantage of you with impunity.

Anyone can fall victim to these strategies. On the surface they come across as reasonable things to ask for in a relationship, but as the expectations pile up the situation worsens. It starts with you going to events with them and then ends with you driving them and their drunken friends home. The genius of their tactic is their ability to phrase everything as utterly normal. This allows them to fool countless amounts of people because they snake their way into others' trust by appearing to be healthy.

You agreed to wedding vows but ended up with a laundry list. There's always more you have to do. After cooking meals, you have to do dishes, after spending all night cleaning, you don't listen enough, if you manage to do all of that then he's worried about how little you go out. There's always judgment, always more for you to accommodate.

No matter what you do, something is wrong and it's your fault. He missed an interview because he didn't have cigarettes, but he didn't buy a pack because you drove in your car last night and you didn't want it to smell like smoke. You never asked him to not buy the cigarettes, but that's not the point. The point was that he was late and you were around, so it's your fault. You need to do more. You should have driven him to the interview.

Everything that goes wrong can be traced back to you. The mental gymnastics of doing so has become part of your daily routine. You've grown accustomed to expecting guilt as soon as you start interacting with him. Conversations generally begin with something you did that caused some problem for him.

At first, it felt fair. He appreciated parts of you but didn't appreciate others. That's how everybody feels about everybody else, it's nothing special. But fter moving in together, that changed soon: all of a sudden there weren't so many positive attributes to you, but there were thousands of flaws. As much as he appreciated you before he criticizes you now.

You tried to change things about yourself, but it was never enough. You stopped going to yoga because it was too revealing of a hobby for someone your age, you stopped going out to eat because it was a foolish way to spend money, and you've stopped even suggesting shows to watch. You know that everything you enjoy he will find stupid, unimportant.

It feels like a sickness, but when you complain to your friends, even when you complain to your mother, they brush it away as one of the problems of getting married. You start to feel a little crazy because this thing that's slowly killing you, making you turn grey from the inside out, is being explained off as the woes of love. How could love be something that takes you so far from yourself?

All day you end up servicing his needs and his hobbies, and at the end you don't even have an hour for yourself. You end up living around the corners of your life, trying to collect pieces of yourself in the scraps that you've been left. For thirty minutes a night, you have the freedom to read what you like. As a silent hobby, it's hard for him to have anything to say about it without doing actual research.

Cleaning yourself at the end of the day becomes a ritual. The greatest feeling is to remove your suit of armor, your second skin of cosmetics. At that moment you know yourself because you can see yourself. That's what you looked like playing in your parents' yard.

You relax as much as you can but stress is still held throughout your body. Your shoulders bunch up. Your back feels like a network of tributaries of knots and pain, your whole body aches for relief.

Baths help your body reset to some sort of average, but you still have a lot of accumulated stress that never really goes away.

You're brave enough to deal with it, you're strong enough to say nothing, but your body doesn't forget. Just because you don't care that you're bleeding doesn't mean that the wound goes away.

When engaged in a relationship like this, it's nothing but toxic. The narcissist is treating you like a slave. Live like this long enough and you will be an extension of them, like a glove. Physical boundaries are an important part of everyone's psychology, and you need to set them up.

In marriage these lines are blurred, for we must make sacrifices for the people that we live around, but that makes establishing them all the more important. Narcissists will never show restraint in how they take from supply, you must make them stop. They don't have a gauge for how much they should take they only notice once you're too exhausted to contribute anything else. Once you are unable of taking care of even yourself, they will let off, but they don't do so to let you recharge.

Once you stop functioning as an ideal supply the narcissist will not understand that you are tired, but think that you're spent, that you've given the best you have to give. Because of this, they will move on and attempt to find another target, someone they can extract more value from.

This will often manifest as affairs. After they have drained their target so much that they seem dull and incapable, they will find them unattractive. Once they do, they will disengage with their target and find something with more potential. Thus, the problem of the younger woman occurs in many marriages.

If this happens it is important not to internalize it. You did not deserve this behavior and it says nothing about the quality of who you are. Obviously, you were attractive enough for them in the beginning. It is through their own mistreatment of you that you grew to stop living up to the standards they wanted you to live up to. You are no lesser than they found you, you are tired, and you are tired because they ran you like a horse. There's nothing you did wrong and nothing you could do better other than respecting yourself and being a better friend to yourself.

To disengage from this dynamic, you must forgive yourself and let go of the guilt. Everything you were blamed for wasn't your fault. Narcissists convince others of guilt that no human could have. You don't control time, or weather, or luck. Realize your innocence before fate and reassess the relationship you want to have with the world. Give to what you value, disassociate from what drains you.

Living this way is difficult because you must put yourself first and be unashamed of your own interest. After living with a narcissist, and especially after being married to one, you may be convinced that you don't have the right to do so, or that it's evil to put yourself first. This isn't the case.

All of us are born alone. All of us have to take care of ourselves. Narcissists know this and live by it, they only shame you out of this truth because they want you to take care of them before you take care of yourself. It is not bad to take care of yourself. You are not taking away attention from anything by doing so. In fact, it's crucial to take care of yourself because if you don't, somebody else has to. Neglecting your needs doesn't make them go away. It just means that you will have them met by ways outside of your control.

So take control of your needs and supply them for yourself. Doing so will grow your independence and confidence. Once you learn how easy it is to live for yourself, and how much more direct problems are when they stem from your action rather than others', you will be more than capable of taking care of yourself. Once you can nurture yourself, then you can extend your energy into the world with a truly positive effect.

Law 10

«Things Must Change, For Better or for Worse»

Aphrodite's Law

If it is a beautiful pain, is it not good?

Drama is the currency, the water in which the narcissists swim. To them, the peak of emotional experience is when they can provoke a grandiose display of feeling, positive or negative, because it proves their importance. They will risk everything, relationships, safety, or security, just to have a moment of interest, to be around someone feeling something or to feel something themselves.

Due to this, they may be cruel, acting in a sadistic manner solely for the rise they can get out of their victim. It is a display of dominance, a way of proving that they own your emotional stability.

Games of power are their essential modus operandi. They don't understand healthy human dynamics, so instead, they try to get control of them, and enforce expression through manipulation rather than pursuing natural expression.

The average person has feelings that are more complicated than they can explain. Someone can express that they're feeling down, but they may not be able to trace it back to the fact that construction is happening on a street that's remained the same for 60 years, and driving through it set them into an exploration of the impermanence of even the most established things. We are influenced by thousands of such subtle stimuli everyday, and to expect us to be able to trace every piece of our feeling back to its cause is foolishness.

Narcissists are in tune with this experience, but only for themselves. They have their own attachment to the world, and their own form of sentimentality, but they cannot perceive that everybody around them has as complicated a relationship with the world as they do. Because of this, they manipulate other people's feelings because they do not see them as legitimate as the feelings they experience.

They cannot relate to the nostalgia of others, but they can understand that it influences others, so they may take advantage of their memory to charm others. If they know that their target has a favorite café or aesthetic, they will make efforts to always be presented in those settings so that it's easier to gain the trust of the person that they are targeting.

Behavior like this is tricky because it mimics someone who listens to you well. The difference is in attitude. If someone cares enough to bring you to places you like it is often because they can relate to your appreciation for it, or because they want to cater to your taste. Both lead to expression, either of mutual appreciation for the setting, or curiosity for what drives your love for the experience.

The narcissist will feel neither of these, but through conversation they will reveal that it was merely something they had memorized about you, not something that they were interested in. Both of those things tend to come together in healthy people. Someone will remember a personal detail about you, but then they will want to expand their understanding of it, and share the experience with you.

The narcissist does not because the narcissist isn't trying to have an experience with you. They're trying to grow their data on you, to learn your emotional triggers, positive and negative, and your relationship to them. They're not trying to explore you. They're trying to map you.

Something to look out for is the one-sided conversation. Just like they can catch you, forcing you to listen to hours of monologues, to study you they will employ the opposite tactic. They will get you talking without contributing much to the conversation. This is so that you reveal yourself completely. The conversation will be going too fast, and it will come across more like speed dating than getting to know somebody.

Once they have a full picture of your psyche then they will be able to play their game. By sketching you out, they've sketched out the boundaries that they are able to push, what works, and what will make you leave them.

The thin ice defines every conversation. You try to smile and continue the relationship, to talk about what you used to and to trust him again, but you remember. You remember that night, even though it was a month ago, when he screamed at you. He screamed until his voice went hoarse. He attacked your weight, your face, your taste in makeup, your closet, your voice, everything. Nothing was sacred.

Now he wants everything to be normal again. You tried to leave, but he talked about how important you were, how real the relationship was. It broke your heart to go so you gave him a second chance, but this isn't the first second chance. You feel afraid to talk, like anything could set him off. It's terrifying, but the sex has been amazing. He's been bringing you out on dates. He's talking about how great you are again. What can you trust?

Everything flips on a dime. You go out on the most architected dates of your life. He remembers what parts of town you like, your dietary habits, and what kind of seating you like. Every date feels like something out of a storybook, you've never felt so flattered.

The conversation during the dates are fine too, normal, polite. You talk about appropriate things, the tones stay low, and everything feels respectful. You start to think this is what it's like to be an adult and deal with romance, that this is the measure everything else should be held to.

At home it's different though. You come in grateful and try to be as pleasing as you can. You wear the things that he likes, you try not to distract conversation onto the topics that he doesn't want to discuss. You try to exude positive energy. The night would be so perfect if it could end how it began.

Eventually, you've said something that he doesn't like. He took it as an attack and so he's yelling about how much he does for you, how much sacrifice he's made for you in his life. You try to preserve your positive attitude, but the mask cracks once he starts beating his chest. Tears stream down your face as the music continues to play in another room.

The fight goes on, him complaining about not being appreciated, you sobbing as you promise that you love him and that you didn't mean anything. It goes on for the better part of 2 hours. Eventually his mood shifts.

Now his hands are on your chin and he's promising you that you're a beautiful and perfect woman. Your face is still wet from your tears. Sweet words fall from his mouth like poison as he kisses the top of your head and holds you in his wiry hands.

You end up in bed together, again. The next day everything is explained away by the emotions of the evening. Your heart feels cold, but he focuses on the sex, how great it felt to be able to sleep with such a beautiful woman after pleasing her.

There's nothing for you to say, really, so you just let him have it. You nod along to his nonsense and let him pretend like everything is okay. Instead of waiting for him, you order a cab home. Once you're back, you cry.

It's been like this for months. You thought it was a hiccup in getting to know each other, but it's gotten no better. Part of you wishes that you had bruises because then there'd at least be something to show when you told others you felt like you were rotting.

This paradigm devalues you to yourself. It makes you comfortable with letting yourself be berated and abused. Children with abusive parents often fall into this paradigm, then face the same abuse as they grow up. Let no one teach you that that is an acceptable way to treat somebody, because that's just programming to be good narcissistic supply.

Love isn't supposed to be a chain. It's not supposed to feel limiting and guilty like there's something wrong with you. If you were taught that you were supposed to behave to receive love, then you were taught by unhealthy people.

Unconditional love isn't a fantasy. It's what every human deserves from somewhere, whether from family or lover is unimportant. There should be no pressure on you to maintain standards to receive the care that humans require for survival. You need people in your life that are willing to help you because you exist, not because they can get something out of you.

Living without unconditional love will convince you that everything in the world is done out of interest. This model works, but for machines and games, not for humans. We cannot simply be judged as good enough and then receive what we need to exist. We must be given what we need to exist, then rise to our highest potential. You can't put the cart in front of the horse.

Establishing this in your life is difficult if you've never had experience with it. Convincing yourself that you deserve it is a hard step for a lot of people, but it's true. We all deserve the opportunity to meet our potential.

You need distance, privacy above all else. There is no telling when another attack is coming, and if you are at risk of it hurting you severely, all the better to cut it off as soon as you can. Stop having sex with them if you are romantically involved. Respect your boundaries physically and emotionally. Defend yourself, and if they won't let you, find a community that will.

Reaching out to new people and forming new relationships may seem very intimidating. This is common for people who have suffered from narcissistic abuse. Many find themselves feeling unlovable and afraid of interacting with the world after being abused.

This is an unfortunate position to be in, but a beatable one. People are better than you think, and the more that you can trust them by giving your time to the community around you, the more that you will benefit. If you live in a city you are especially well equipped to make more connections, but if you are isolated or shy, there are plenty of internet communities to consider.

What you need to focus on is finding healthy relationships with a common interest. This does not mean finding someone else who likes pottery, but it may. What it means is finding people who want to engage with the world in the same ways that you do. If you want to volunteer six hours a week to teaching children pottery, then the people who also choose to do so will probably have values that align with your own.

By associating with people like that, you expose yourself to situations in which you may bond with healthy social networks, becoming a part of something that will give back to your life more than what you give to it. This will give you a secure form of support for yourself and your interests, so when someone else tries to take away your ability to stand up for yourself you will remember who you're standing up for.

Law 11

«You Will Be Told to Mourn the Living»

Hades' Law

Everything goes, so respect this home.

Another way for the narcissist to gain influence over the lives of others is pity. Most of us share a natural concern for the sick and the disadvantaged, so we will make time to tend to those who seem to be hurt or oppressed. The narcissist is aware of that, so they will appear to be suffering to gain influence over our hearts, and to gain access to the attention we reserve for the most disadvantaged in our society.

In morose moods, the narcissist may obsess about death, or the temporary nature of all things. Many old maids have rocked in chairs on porches telling their relatives, "You know I'm not going to be here forever". This focus on the common fate of all things isn't a true reflection on mortality, but a self-centered statement that they won't be here forever, so you should appreciate them while they last.

We all must come to grips with the fact that our lives are ending. Every second you spend living means that you are a second closer to your death. For healthy people, this doesn't mean that life is a punishment. In fact, many of us are able to come to a point where we celebrate the journey. We all understand that it will end, of course, but we also see that we might as well appreciate what we have.

The narcissist does not hold onto this conception, though. They act like the mourning mother of a soldier killed in battle, acting the part of fallen soldier and mother both. This is because they have little to no actual understanding of our mortality. They developed a death fetish.

This obsession with death, pain, or weakness paints the narcissist in the light of a victim, which is a position they know how to abuse well. When someone is disadvantaged in our society, we are not left cold. We care. We want to see them have the right to stand on their own feet and lead happy lives.

Because of this the narcissist knows that they can extract resources from someone who pities them. They will attempt to get their targets to disregard their time and responsibility in the face of the difficulties of their life. Everything will be dramatized so that they can gain better access to the resources of others.

By doing this, the victim let themselves be stolen from. It may literally manifest economically, where through pity the narcissist tries to extract meals, money, and other favors, especially such as obtaining addictive substances. Using their story as a smokescreen, they will find justification for partaking in the worst actions conceivable. They will remind you of their plight once you catch onto their plans.

There are leagues of issues for them to fall back on because, once you're lying, it's easy to have every problem in the world. An anxiety issue can be turned into a stomach issue. A sprained ankle might be turned into back pain. Everything can be blurred when the symptoms aren't there, so then any condition can become any other.

It's hard to catch them in the lie because then you will have to go against the human instinct to help. You will have to delegitimize their complaints and tell them that being hurt does not give you the right to hurt others. Doing so will trigger a fight, and you will have to be able to stand your ground.

This is one of the most unfair positions that a narcissist will force you into. They will make you have to call out someone for faking their conditions, which is a cruel action, but there's nothing to do with a liar but know that they're lying and be unafraid to say so.

He will find any excuse to complain that you don't have enough time for him. You rack your brain and try to see how that's true considering you live together, but then you remember that you work, you go to school, and you're the only one who cleans the house. You apologize, but he continues to sulk, so you skip class to try to cheer him up.

For two hours you sulk with him, his mood seemingly unchanged. You try to meet him at his energy, but end up lost in a mire of cynicism and self-defeating attitudes. He got laid off two weeks ago, so he has more time. All of that time is spent at home, dreaming about being famous or successful, but doing nothing other than complaining. Your energy begins to die.

As someone dear to him, you're expected to go along with his fantasies, to give substance to his air drumming, and other navel-gazing hobbies. Every day you have to listen to his plans to go into certain occupations, or finalize certain connections, but there's no time left for how you want to support yourself. When you talk about your degree that's too boring, you harp about yourself too much, but he's buying pieces for a drum set that lays unused in the garage. You wonder how things got so pathetic.

He's always going on and on about what he could be, if only he had the money, if only his dad would help him, if only something. There's always a block between him and his goals, and nothing he can see to do about it. At the end of the day he promises that he wants nothing more than to take care of you, but the dishes pile up, the floors get dirty, and the laundry lies wrinkled in the dryer.

An easy life on the horizon is what he always promises, but you can't live in a mirage. You need to get your life together and put yourself first. Happiness is found through taking care of yourself and having a well-balanced life, so you need dependability, not dreams.

You try to explain this to him, but then the pity seeps into the room again. You're forgetting his back pain, his anxiety, his trauma, and anything else that can be leveraged to bulldoze over your point of view. Instead of listening to you and your needs, he will try to gain dominance over the conversation.

To do so everything from his life is brought up again. You can't remember how many times he's brought up his parents' divorce. Everyone has problems, and you truly felt for his, but now they're a facet of your everyday life. There is nothing that you can do to make it better, nothing that he will do to make it better, just the continual conversation about how hard life is for him, and how difficult it is for him to function. Essentially, arguments for why he has the right to remain a child.

When you push against this you either have to deal with a pouting adult, or an adult throwing a tantrum. Both are embarrassing to communicate with and leave you with no interest in standing up for yourself, because the fight he wants to fight is undignified. He wants his stench to be enough for you to love and protect him, but we all rot. We all have problems, and we all must rise above them.

If this is not understood as a human, there will be serious issues that crop up. Problems are a quintessential part of the human experience and to attempt to ignore them is to attempt to opt out of part of the gift. Life was given to us misshapen and imbalanced, not perfect. To live well you must be able to know how to fall, even the best among us cannot always stay on their feet.

The risk of living around someone poisoned like this is that they will influence you into becoming a mummy. If you allow someone to mourn life around you every day that influence will seep into you and numb you to life too. You will not be able to enjoy seeing your country's flag at the Olympics, nor silly pop music that makes you want to dance.

Their apathy seeps through the bones like tar. It is easy to be ungrateful for life, and once you start you risk falling into a downward spiral that ends with nihilism or cynicism.

Happiness is not how some people wake up, it is a harmony that all of must find by ourselves with life. It's a deal you must strike with your environment to make peace with it. To find inner harmony you must create distance between yourself and the triggers that you find yourself suffering from being exposed to.

If you find too difficult to defend yourself against pity, then you must accept that and become hardened to it. People can move into your life through that instinct and drain you. It is better to be closed off and learning how to open up than it is to be completely open. Once you give something to someone, they will often think that there is more to score from you.

Trace what influences you. Journal about your uncomfortable experiences and find what causes them. It might be something as simple as you feel uncomfortable around people in suits. The problem might also be incredibly subtle, like that you can't deal with people who sound like they've been crying without giving them all the help that you can give. Either way, you should start to feel out your psychology and record your habits. Once you have a good understanding of that, identifying the things about yourself that obstruct you from embracing life will come naturally.

To find the way out of the scars the narcissist left, you must simply stop listening to them. Every time they open up with world hating monologues either tune out or leave. Refuse to let that philosophy into your life. Let your appreciation for life dominant, and respect the time, space, and silence you need to keep faith.

Once you start the journey towards healing yourself and becoming whole, there is no stopping. You cannot turn back or let yourself slip, this work is crucial to the development of your personality, and your soul. By not finishing your work of striking your own deal with life, you will fall back into letting someone else define your experience, and this is one of the least fulfilling ways to live.

Narcissists are not strong, they appear to be. The confidence that they exude is not natural. They don't deserve to be so sure of themselves. You may be convinced that they are competent people, but they are not. Their excellence in one area does not excuse a poor attitude, or self-pity. Nobody gets what they deserve in life, they get what they can secure.

Narcissists disagree, however, and believe that they deserve special treatment. They think that other people exist to dote on them and to make their experience in this life comfortable. Misery does no better in company. Do not fall into their trap of rejecting the world. There is no healing it, there is only being lost further to the numbness.

Law 12

«You Will Be Told They Know Better»

Athena's Law

Without guidance potential is nothing.

One of the delusions of the narcissist stems from their tastes. Their taste is often impeccable, which leads them to believe that they have a part in developing the quality of the things they enjoy. When a narcissist shares incredible intimacy with you it most often comes with the opinion that they have a positive influence on your development. Occasionally narcissists suffer from the negative manifestation of disorder, being sure they cannot do anything positive in their lives, but either way, they will try to convince you that either you need them, or they need you. It's not important which role they play. It is the creation of this dynamic that is unhealthy.

They are trying to make their access to you permanent: once you are responsible for each other, this is a bond that will never be broken. Because of this, the narcissist will try dominate your professional life, either by jockeying control over your business, or trying to get you to work within their own. This power relationship grows habitual over time, leaving you unsure of what to do without them, or feeling awful for not giving them the support they have made you accustomed to giving.

This relationship also allows them to be covert because they can hide behind occupational and economic necessities. Instead of looking like they're trying to control your schedule and your time, they can play it off as wanting the best for both of you, as trying to secure your future. When they can frame it this way, it makes you more accommodating of their encroachment into your professional and emotional space.

If you are caught in this dynamic you are in danger. Everyone needs to have independence in their ability to take care of themselves financially. This means being the sole arbiter of your income. There should be no one that you need to work with: if you make clothing you don't need the designer that you work with, you need a competent designer. That could be anyone in the market with enough skills.

Likewise, you should manage your relationships similarly. The point is not to be inhuman and know that everyone in your life is replaceable, but to be at peace with the fact that no matter who you lose you can carry on, just as the people who love you will have to after you pass.

So if there is a circumstance in which you feel that you cannot create as you want to without the influence of a specific person, examine that relationship. There is a possibility that you have engaged in worship, and that you have idealized this person. This is not the worst problem to have, and it can be solved through acclimating to a more grounded standard, but if the person that you feel attached to is a narcissist, things will be more complicated.

You may have been convinced of this reliance through demonstration. Perhaps they helped you develop a talent or break through to a market with the skills that you already possess. It might have been great support for you to receive, but it is important to note that the victory was your own. No one else is responsible for your success other than you, and people who try to take that from you don't actually care about you.

There was a time when you were making $120 a month off your online business selling artistic trinkets. They were tasteful things some people would love to have around. You were happy with it and dreamed of the success it would become, but decided to keep your job and throw time into the trinkets as a hobby. Then your husband promised that he could make it your full-time gig and he took over the marketing. You received several orders for the same project, a dilemma which he suggested you fix by making replicas of the same piece.

The business took off and you stayed up later making the same things over and over. You cut your store down to five items and spent all the time you weren't working on that. It lasted a month and you ended up making double the money, but you quit because it wasn't your business. You wanted to be selling things that were unique. You ended up making disposable stuff. It wasn't the dream you had in mind.

After that you lost interest. You no longer were moved by the little things you kept around your house, the rocks from Joshua Tree, or the feathers from Missouri. They don't look like enjoyable memories anymore, they looked like money. You pack them all up into crates you can't see through, and then you shove them in the attic.

For a while life continues on with the rhythm of things. Going to work, making meals, seeing some shows, all of those things pass by as the seasons die. Life is fine, you're doing things you like, but its production and consumption.

In the spring you find a guitar sitting around in the vinyl shop. It has layers of dust on it. On the body of it are a few bumper stickers from the 80s. You show it to the clerk and ask about it, he says he will let go of it for $20.

That night you're practicing in your bedroom, finding songs that you used to sing while you were getting your license. It feels like flying to play around again, to feel your body expand past the physical realm that we're all married to. Weeks go by and you feel freedom with every new chord that you learn, every chorus that naturally flows from you.

You decide to post some of the covers you do to YouTube. It's not the most original idea, but it's just for you anyway. After a few months you earn a couple thousand subscribers. People think you have some things to pick up in terms of playing guitar, but most of them love your voice. A community starts to form around your work, active with every video that you post. Another season goes by and you start to post your original work every week. Finally, you're starting to feel back in touch with the world, like you can communicate again.

Your husband finds the channel. He's incredibly excited, and you fall for it. You get excited that he's excited and show him everything, the documents full of lyrics, the songs you've yet to record, and your channel analytics. His eyes sparkle at the numbers.

He starts to give you suggestions, how you should do your hair, and what songs you should play. You go along with it at first because you just want something to share with him. His advice works, the numbers double after you clean up and play a simple song that's on the radio.

He's so proud of you. The next week he has another song suggestion. Again, the process continues, your numbers grow, it turns into a real opportunity, but you don't even want to hold the instrument anymore. You want to be left alone. Even in your bedroom you feel the hungry gaze of strangers. All you want is an outlet, not to become one.

Being open to criticism is great. Letting yourself be a doormat for other peoples' standards and ideas is an awful idea. It'll lead you nowhere and you will end up hating what you were doing in the first place.

Narcissists are dangerous influences because they are indirect with their intentions. When they appear to be communicating with interest they rarely are, almost every action done by a narcissist is for some advantage. If they take an interest in what you're doing it is more likely that they see that a profit is possible from the endeavor, not that they see the beauty in your undertaking.

Their obsession with taste should not come across as flattery. That is one of the silver linings of being a target of narcissistic abuse, it means you're a very attractive person for one reason or another, but that's a joke we make in the face of incredible pain. The way that a narcissist looks at your value is inhuman, and attracting their interest is a very risky position to be in.

They will not better your relationship with your talents or the world around you. If they make you feel more productive, it is because they are running you to the ground, treating you like a factory. This is not how people treat one another. This is how somebody treats their oil pump from which they want to extract the most resources from.

We are not machines, and so we can't accommodate their standards. By living with the dehumanizing standards of the narcissist your connection to life will be lost, and you will be turned into a resource. If stress is a killer, this is the way to taunt it.

The outside world is a great cure for most conditioning. When you want to have your own journey into your interests and passions, do not be afraid to share them with new people, or people you know deserve your trust. We all need feedback, but we don't need masters. The only master is existence, so do your best to be a part of it. The more honestly you can do that the more trauma will be washed away from you.

Once you can start enjoying what you're doing with your life, then you can start developing your own relationship with independence. If you start on this journey first it may seem too daunting, which is why it's recommended to meet good influences before trekking out on your mission to repair your spirit.

After you have found people with lifestyles that you respect, the ways of love and hate will be more obvious to you. It is possible to make money through both, through love for what is around you, and through hate. Narcissists make money through hate because they make money by gaming the things around them, by manipulating them for advantage.

It is just as possible to find ways to contribute to the world, monetarily or not, through love. If you exude authenticity you will find a place in the world for you to spread your appreciation and interest in anything. The only thing you need to do is communicate that interest by partaking in the world and making sure that it knows that you want to be a part of it.

When you extend a foot into the world you are taking the best part of the burden. You are communicating your willingness to take risks, to give up your time for something outside of yourself. Such a statement will not go unheard. If you can commit to doing this, then you will find a place for yourself, no matter where you go.

Law 13

«You Will Be Treated Like the Enemy»

Aries' Law

All is fair, for I am forever war.

Manipulation isn't the sin of the narcissist, it's the language. They don't feel remorse for using it because they are conditioned to use it. For many narcissists this is due to past trauma. They grew up in, or were exposed to, environments that were so hostile they had to adapt to gaming them to survive. We can attempt to understand them, but we cannot permit their attitude as an appropriate reaction to life.

If we do then they will take liberties with their control of the atmosphere. Once they have a say they want things to be structured around manipulative tactics. They want to create an environment similar to that of war. Everything will become fair game because they recognize no boundaries other than their own.

This means that arguments can start and stop at a moment's notice. For hours they might be calm, and then they might blow up for the rest of the night, sleeping finally at 2 in the morning while seething. Often, when given trust, narcissists become utterly unpredictable. They understand that they won't lose you no matter how they behave, so they test the limits of your loyalty. It's partly to learn how much they can take from others, and partly enjoyment.

They really are incompetent people, so they continually set up rigged situations. They might be incredibly hostile and competitive. If they want you to fight with them, they will want you to fight a certain way. This is because they're trying to elicit a reaction from you, there's not authentic engaging with your feelings. All the feelings that you go through will either be entertainment or annoyance for them.

Situations like this leave you restrained. They're attracted to conflict and drama, but they have no skills to deal with either. This means they are continually pressuring situations to erupt that they can force control over, but they have no idea how to use that control.

Arguments are a natural part of a healthy life. No one should just agree with their significant other, that's how we lose out on an interesting personality. To stand up for yourself is a divine right of being, and something everyone should exercise. Do not let yourself be forgotten.

However, not all arguments are created equally. Healthy arguments end up being about listening. Emotions may rise and things might get hectic, feet can get stepped on and feelings can get hurt, but ultimately that's not the resolution. It resolves because, even when you're pushed past the point that your patience can process, you still want to listen to the ones you love.

After the argument you remember things that they said, and they remember things that you said. With space, both people are able to internalize the other's position, then come together again with more understanding and a wish to make amends. These arguments present no risks to relationships, and in fact are part of the struggles that strengthen them. They are centered on mutual care.

A narcissist will not preserve such healthy balance in their arguments. They will raise their voice but criticize you for raising your own. They will probably not support their arguments, while demanding a precise explanation for every point you make. They will expect your respect while giving you none.

This dynamic is incredibly unfair because it trains you to fight and it trains you to lose. When your parents take the liberty to behave like this, most people have to go on a journey of self-discovery to learn what it is to assert themselves. By living like this, you are being trained to have a poor defense.

Conversations between friends and lovers are supposed to be comfortable. Yet home feels like a minefield and nothing you say seems to make anything better. You try to bring up events going on around town. He questions the event then tries to find another. You ask why you can't go to that one. He asks why you have to go out at all. Nothing is easy, you aren't listened to like an adult, you're stuck arguing like children. That's all that happens when you talk. You tried apologizing and simply listening, but that didn't make anything better.

The way you tell jokes is too crass for him. He doesn't like when you talk about privates because it doesn't sound ladylike. Joking about that stuff is below you, although he's quick to mention his equipment in lieu of a punch line.

Over time your personality has been folded another way. There was someone who used to be spicy, who would tell jokes that would make your friends blush, but you don't remember what it's like to be her. Instead you feel afraid of talking about anything that's not covered by critics in some magazine that doesn't have too many photos.

This attitude has grown to be a part of you, like a shell. It keeps out stares and empty words, but you've spent so much time behind it you've forgotten what's out there. Life seems stale when it's so protected. Everything has numbed into a fog that rolls from one day into the next. Your body responds to your commands, but you don't know what your mind is doing.

Your memory starts to shrink. It's hard to imagine long sentences or places that you've visited in the past. When you wake up in the morning your body feels weak and sick without any apparent reason. You deal with it silently because you don't trust attention from anyone else. It doesn't fade and you grow to expect it to be the way that you will feel for the rest of your life. It's like hell, but there's nothing to do other than continue.

These physical manifestations are real. Mind and body are directly connected. If you are drained and trained to be afraid then you will feel exhausted. Unfortunately, this is convenient for the narcissist because it weakens their victim further, separate from their active manipulation. When they push you to the point of feeling ill, it is much harder to resist them.

Although it sounds dramatic, it is a literal possibility and reality for many people. If you have noticed an acute drop in health shortly after starting to live with a partner, moving back in with your parents, or a change in management, it may be due to a narcissist draining you. Your energy is used to preserve all of your health, body and soul and If there is something draining it your general wellbeing will suffer a lot.

This hostile mode of behavior is most likely the trigger for a lot of narcissists growing up. When someone is always fighting with you like this you may find that your own voice is deteriorating and that you can't get along with anyone. Don't panic if that is the case, it's very difficult to keep your head around this kind of energy.

Along with the physical manifestations of being exposed to this level of stress, there are all sorts of mental problems that can develop as well. For example, trust issues are found in many of the people who have suffered from the exposure to narcissistic people, along with legitimate cases of PTSD.

Narcissists aren't mean; they're people with personality disorders that will hurt you. It's not a phase they're going to grow out of. There is no help for them unless they genuinely want to gain control over their actions, which is rare. More common are narcissists pretending to resolve issues to look like they are making an effort to get better.

They will take superficial opportunities to better themselves, commit to them for long enough to say that they tried. It will be hard to read these efforts as fraudulent because they will put effort into presenting them as genuine, but underneath the display there will be no substance, no real change.

Despite their anger management classes and their mindfulness exercises, you will still be yelled at. Maybe not the first week, or the third, but it will happen again. Narcissists don't hear no, they hear not now.

If there are people you can trust, people you've known for a long time that have a good idea of what you love about yourself, get in contact with them. See if you can spend time together in person and how it affects your mood.

When you're not able to access such relationships then find a place you will feel comfortable in. Find someone who will go to cafés with you, call up an old professor, or find a therapist. Be around people who won't be hostile. That's the most essential point. Try to acclimate yourself to environments in which you don't need to be afraid. Once you can relax then you can flourish again.

If you must live with the narcissist try to not listen. Hear what they say but don't internalize it. Disconnect them from your empathy. Find people that you can express yourself with that don't turn everything into bickering. Engage with positivity. The more you have this energy in your life the less you will hold onto the stress. Your body reacts to what it's used to. If you're used to fighting, it will be tense. If you get used to being comfortable, it will relax.

Have faith in yourself and your ability to heal. Humans are incredibly resilient creatures. We are lucky that we can be hurt so much and still somehow manage to survive. Appreciate that, and don't mourn the time you've lost, invest in a future that you want to see.

Law 14

«They Either Give You Undying Support or Try to Take Home Away from You»

Poseidon's Law

When the waters rage, there is no path home.

Narcissists can come from every facet of life. Whether they are your husband, wife, boss, parent, friend, or teacher they can find a way to damage your reputation. It's not that they manipulate you, it's that they manipulate everyone they can influence, you just may be someone they give a lot of attention. This doesn't mean that they help you or support you. It means that you're an object of interest.

The more important you are in a narcissist's life the more dangerous the relaitonship is, especially when things start to go wrong (and they will). If you quit a job because of an awful boss expect her to attempt to sabotage you as much as she can, up to getting you blacklisted from the industry. If you divorce your husband because of his narcissistic tendencies expect all of your mutual connections to hear his story long before you feel ready to talk about it.

They do not conceive you as an independent human. Worst case scenario they consider you an object, a resource, and at best they see you as a sort of pet. For them love is walking next to their inferior, watching how they react to the things around them. It's a detached experience. It's more of a fascination, they like the way you look instead of being interested in the character. This is true especially when you're dealing with a male narcissist.

This means you are at risk of being destroyed like an old high school journal once you will try to leave on your own accord. He mapped your destinations, he knows where you will be going, and he will attempt everything he can to sabotage every step of your journey.

For them this is as easy as a phone call, a mother crying to an old boss that you would have liked to use as a reference. It is easy to destroy you once you try to gain independence, especially because at the beginning of your journey you will be extremely vulnerable. But if you don't break free then you will never achieve any meaningful goal in your life.

The other option is to do nothing and just decay. If you leave your life in the hands of people who detest you, that are jealous of you, or that treated you like you were their possession, then there will be no journey. Out of spite they will isolate you. Narcissist resent anyone having success in life, especially those who they think have wronged them. They will always blame you for something, whether it's for taking a can of cola from the fridge when you were a child, or for the way you park the car at night. Anything inconsequential can be exacerbated into a sin.

This is because narcissists are failures. No matter the measure of success in their lives, they are hollow. They can't reach a feeling of being whole so they think there's nothing to look for in the world. Due to their own disinterest in the world around them they start to devalue everything and thus cut themselves off from opportunities to grow and achieve real, lasting success. Rather than trying to learn from the people that have healthy relationships with the world, they want to drag the healthy ones down to their level, and keep all of humanity wallowing in its own resentful filth.

Narcissists haze their victims to gain their trust. As you try to leave, they will try hazing you again through abuse. If you line up to their idea of how they think you should act they will accept you back, laughing as they look down at you, thinking that your return is an acceptance of them being correct.

Unfortunately, when narcissists influence our living conditions, the best thing to do is to appease them. It's a survival tactic. Don't fall into their games of guilt or let yourself empathize with their self-obsession, but say the words they want to hear from you, pretend to be the person they want you to be. It's the best way to get through without risking major damage in your life.

The long-term game is to make an exit strategy. Plan a trip to family if you need to break up, find a new roommate if you need to have a talk, or reach out to your community before leaving an abuser. Once you go don't look back. That will only cause problems.

There is no adequate reason to go back. If you gloat about your success, you will ruin it. If you want to pacifically end the relationship you will always be approaching it without reaching it. If you want to help them find peace your goodwill will be misused. The journey must be away from them, if they're willing to destroy your exit then they're people you should never be around under any circumstance.

To commit to your direction, commit to your life. Follow new occupational opportunities, move, and fully engage in a hobby. Learn a new language. Keep finding new spaces to occupy, ledges to grip, during your ascent away from the people trying to hold you down.

This will be the same weight as becoming independent from your parent if the relationship has gone far enough. It will feel like stepping out into the world unprepared, but every awkward step you take will strengthen you.

Once you have gone far enough from them, the domains will change. You will be a stranger in a new land, but that's better than being under the thumb of someone who wants to control you. You will have to grow accustomed to new standards, or if you're lucky enough, return to healthy standards in a place you've lived before. The longer you commit to this the more natural it will be for you to either resettle, or to travel.

There's nothing wrong with going nomadic, especially if you need space to find yourself. Explore the world and find new standards. Odysseus stayed on a single island for a decade. There is a time in your life where you need to stop, and explore places where you haven't been before. You will fall in love again, and you will be hurt again, but that's what it feels like to be human and it's okay. The more comfortable that you become with it, the less that it will hurt.

Law 15

«To Create Demand, Supply Must be Cut»

The Law of Famine

Food tastes better when starved.

Scarcity is one of the driving principles behind value, and with the objectifying perspective of the narcissist, this can be abused to warp your perception of them. A common strategy for them is to leave just as you grow comfortable with them, or start to learn how they are taking advantage of you. It feels like you might never see them again. After months, you might even move on. The most common time for them to return is either right when you feel better or right when you have an unbearable longing for them.

This strategy is so effective because throughout their relationship with their victim they feed them just enough pieces of kindness for them not to leave. By doing so, they affect the release of oxytocin in the body, which is a chemical responsible for positive moods. The victim is acclimated to so much negativity from the narcissist that when the narcissist acts normally to them, by holding the door for them, or by helping them with a chore, their body releases the same oxytocin that it would if someone did something great for them. Over time, the standards held by an individual are denigrated so much that the narcissist barely has to lift a finger to invoke appreciation from his victim.

Narcissists are not perfect, obviously, and sometimes they are too cruel, forcing the illusion they cast over their victim to break. When this happens, they will withdraw, realizing that they have pushed the boundaries too far. They will distract themselves with other opportunities, and then return once they can sense their victim is not nervous anymore.

If the victim's trust doesn't return, then the narcissist will either turn to an argument, playing on the emotions of their target, or abandon them again. Either way, they will fall back immediately on manipulation instead of authentically engaging with their victim. Their only concern about the emotions of their victim is how much this will affect his plans.

The more effort they're convinced that it will take to manipulate the person, the more likely they will be to move on. Otherwise, going no contact is a great strategy. By allowing them no access to your life you can be completely free from their manipulation. It will allow you to think straight again. The most important part is to return to your voice, and your interactions with the world around. Train yourself to be proud of making your bed, not of being able to skate by an abusive person without being yelled at. Rewire yourself to reward yourself over rewarding the toxic people around you.

If you continue to trust them and continue to stay under their influence then your standards will not be reset. The victim of narcissistic abuse has an oxytocin response that mimics the way how HSPs process the world around them. It is an oversensitivity to the world, but for the victim of narcissistic abuse, there is no silver lining. HSPs benefit from a depth of emotional insight and a proclivity to profound thinking, but the victims of narcissistic abuse have lower standards than they need to maintain for a happy life. Granted that it takes less to make them happy, but that is because true happiness has been withheld from them for so long. There is no benefit to starving, even if it improves the taste of every meal.

Things had finally been settled. Your schedule aligned with your diet, your habits were healthy and accommodating, you appreciated the free time that you had, and your work was bearable. Living with him started rough, but it was working out. He wasn't staying up as late watching TV so loud, you weren't arguing about semantics, and it looked like everything was going to even out.

Tuesday morning you woke up and he was gone. You had a text that said he had to go, he needed to be refreshed. With no idea where he was going you hoped it wouldn't end up with him back at the psych ward. Trying to keep your pace, you go through the circuit of your schedule. You attempt to keep the anxiety at bay, but it feels like your stomach is filled with battery acid.

He will return again and you will have to find your center all over. There is no stability in this lifestyle, nothing that you can build on. Do not be a free resource, or else you will be establishing your worth as nothing. If you want to let a narcissist back in your life again, because you truly do care about them and cannot go through with complete separation, then the least you can do is to make them earn your time and respect. The worst thing to do is to communicate that you will always be available: they will remember that, and use it as an excuse to drain you to your last drop.

It's best to defend against this by not letting them have any influence on your schedule or decision making. If they want to spend time with you make them take you to a concert or go to a museum that you enjoy. Do things on your terms too, don't let someone return with a set of standards. Stand up for yourself and be independent. If you don't, and you let predators remain in your life, you will be hunted.

They target people for their lack of self-care. Any sort of disadvantage is attractive to them because it furthers the advantages of scarcity. If you have an issue with affirmation, or self-love, then the narcissist can prey on that, feed you false positivity, and capitalize on your positive reaction.

This is a terrible thing to realize when studying the psychology of abuse victims. Many people exit abusive situations with codependency issues, meaning that they rely on things outside of themselves to find balance. Narcissists prey on this instinct and target the weakest among us as their victims because they are the most vulnerable to their attacks.

This is why committing to yourself is so crucial. If you allow any avenue open to the world that you don't know how to properly control, then the narcissist will use that against you for manipulative effect. Do not depend on them for anything, help yourself.

Cutting yourself off from the world may feel unnatural, but sometimes you have to cover up to avoid the rain. It's better to feel stuffy and limited than it is to get sick, and it will only be until you can get back inside. Defend yourself by keeping yourself cared for. You are the best resource in this war.

Law 16

«Punishment Will be Given to Those Who do not Listen and Obey»

The Law of Pestilence

If this land will not accept god, then it will suffer.

Narcissists suffer from black and white thinking. This manifests in different ways, but often in the form of pro and contra, meaning a mindset where things are either on their side or against them. They invest a lot of energy into what they think is good, or on their side, and trying to make sure it succeeds. Likewise, if something falls into the category of things they perceive as against themselves, then they will do a lot to inflict misery on it.

Working from this mindset, they see no reason not to wound those that they see as failing. Most often this will manifest in covert behavior, as narcissists like to keep their work clean. An example is scheduling a meeting with a professor the day you needed a ride to an interview, after you were fired from your current job for being late. You were late because you were hungover, but you were hungover because when you get yelled at you tend to drink.

That's not how he internalizes it though. He sees you as a drunkard, and deserving to suffer the consequences. In his opinion, your negative decisions deserve to be felt through your life, thinking that you will change as the world wears you down. So he continually takes away support from you, spreads rumors that you won't be able to trace, and digs at you with indirect comments.

This energy is incredibly unhealthy to be around because it's shifting guilt onto you. All of us have struggles with life, but that's to be expected. Humans are fallible creatures; we suffer from the imbalances within ourselves and our history. That's part of the experience, and we grow from it.

To identify behaviors like this a strategy you can implement is to feed the narcissist false information. By telling them about hobbies you're not actually attached to, and interests you don't have, you can watch how they attack these things. They may begin to talk them down in front of you, or tell derogatory jokes about them around your mutual connections, but either way, whatever they do they will reveal their strategies to you. Once you can see them played out on things that aren't emotional triggers for you, you will be able to trace back the way that they treated the things that you do care about.

When you're aware of this you will be able to perceive the abuse that they subject you to. By doing so, you can then identify what they're encroaching on and start defending against it. Understanding their strategies and how they affect you is crucial in breaking free from their influence. They study their victims intensely, so the longer you've been exposed to them the more detailed of a map they possess of your psychology. Once you see how they traverse your psychology, you can then limit their access.

If you have no defenses, they will be able to corrupt your soul. Their poison is powerful, and it spreads. Exposure to it, especially when they want to punish you, can strip you of your personality. It is a direct threat to your health.

Break free from the channels of access they have to you and secure relationships with healthier tributaries. Make sure to focus on the healthy influences in your life and limit those that you can feel in your gut are bad for you.

He's gotten sharper and sharper with his comments, explaining to you all the things you don't understand about life due to your physical characteristics. At first those physicals characteristic were amazing, back when you were a trophy. Now they're flaws. You're his underappreciated dog, locked in your kennel.

In the beginning narcissists study their targets, trying to analyze as much as they can so that they can earn the trust of their victims. As time goes on, once the targets dependent on the narcissists, often through living situations, the narcissists will flip the information they uncovered to abuse the people they used to shower affection on. This is because their understanding of you is shallow. They're using the things that they used to praise you for against you because they don't know anything else about you.

Don't interpret this as an issue with you. Realize that you're being targeted by someone who doesn't care about you. Detach from that voice at all costs, you don't deserve to constantly be criticized. That's one of their favorite strategies, to pick you apart through the guise of logic. This is a gross and detached way to gain dominance over their target.

Your psyche is formed by the accumulative experiences in your life, so by being in environments where someone is always chipping at you, you will be broken down. He will take from you like the sea takes from the cliffs, every moment of every day. It may take a while, but all will disappear.

To get out of this, you need to insist on the things that you value. Cook how you want to, go to visit places how you want to, experience life as you want to. Take the freedom that you deserve and don't let somebody else's clouds ruin your day. You are the person who will have to live with yourself for the rest of your life, so make sure that you're somebody you're proud to be.

It's bad to be selfish and cut yourself off from the world, but ultimately only your opinion matters when it comes to how you spend your time. Do what you enjoy and what you think contributes to your future. Don't subscribe to things outside of yourself. Trust what you can build. Invest in the reality that you can manifest. It's how you gain independence.

So, just as they chip at you over time, taking bits out of you, add to yourself again, piece by piece. Repair your relationship with yourself by spending your time taking care of you instead of anything else. Little things become huge over time. Cooking for yourself, cleaning the spaces that you need, and otherwise being on your own side will provide you with an incredible ally. The more that you've done in the past for yourself, the more you will benefit.

A house isn't built in a day, it takes weeks. This is because you have to be careful with the work. You have to make sure that it will last. Take all the time that it needs to do it right, and then you won't have to do it again. It's better to spend your resources on building something up, and then to be able to keep it, than it is to spend time on something that falls apart. Build yourself up as secure as you can. It will protect you from everything.

Law 17

«The Center of Your Life Will be Shifted Towards Them»

The Law of Worth

Value is perceived, so what is yours without me?

As empaths are inherently externally emotive creatures, they often lack strong internal values and self-value. This makes narcissistic attitudes attractive, as there is so much self-image, so much importance, and so much presence in their energy that the empaths feel like the narcissists understands things about life that they do not.

Because of this some people mistake narcissistic abuse for a 'narcissist and empath' cycle - meaning that individuals fall in between the identities over time. This is a misunderstanding of both conditions: one is a personality disorder, and the other is a category of HSP. Both are studied and confirmed through research. A narcissist cannot become an empath, and an empath cannot become a narcissist.

What can occur is imitation. Covert narcissists study HSPs, and empaths, to learn their behaviors. They do this to build a convincing mask of a caring person. Without the knowledge of how to set up and maintain healthy relationships, they simply copy the strategies of those who do.

This does not mean that the narcissist is an empath or is becoming empathic. They're just using the tools of others. Their interest is not in learning how to treat people better, or how to take part of something they weren't included in, it's to learn how to fly under people's concern for danger.

On the other hand, empaths may imitate narcissists. After being exposed to their energy, or in the midst of it, they may take on narcissistic behavior just as they take on attributes of everyone around them. If the narcissist had a deep influence on the empath then the empath may have a deep impression from them, and so they may imitate their behavior extensively. An example of this is an empath who grew up in a narcissistic household.

After being submerged in negative examples throughout the most impressionable part of their life, the empath may pick up habits such as insisting on their point of view, fact-checking everything, and blocking out new informations. The difference is that, when the empath integrates this behavior, it is out of defense, not to manipulate others. They are trying to reestablish their control over themselves, so they are fighting back instinctively with the tools that have been used against them. To be cured from this conditioning they simply need to be removed from the narcissists in their lives and to be introduced to more healthy standards.

For all people, exposure to narcissists will upset the focus of their life. Narcissists continually dig for more attention, more access to resources, anything that they can squeeze out of the people around them.

This is why it's essential to create and maintain distance from them. If there is any point of access they have into your life, then they will use that to shift you back to them, to use you as supply.

You never thought of yourself as a great singer, but you loved being part of a band. Your band had formed in high school and it was very fun. Sometimes you played, sometimes you got drunk, but always you got along. It was just a piece of life.

Gradually the band fell apart, people moved away, and you went to college. After a semester there, you started hanging out with this producer, someone who made electronic music. He had you do vocals for him. The songs got popular enough to play at some small festivals. He said you were going to be famous. You got to go up on stage. It was amazing. You crowd surfed. You never felt so plugged in performing before.

Unfortunately though, you didn't want to date him, not even after all that. He accepted the no, but then stopped calling you. You never got to go back to his studio. You never worked together again. When you saw him, he asked how the singing was going. Eventually you just learned to ignore him, and you finished your degree.

Years later he checks in on you, asking how things are going. You answer honestly, but you feel his dry judgment over every word that you say. Once you've told him your story, he responds with his, both trying to humble himself by saying he's been living just like you, and by sharing magical stories of parties straight out of *The Great Gatsby*.

The phone call drags on until you find an excuse to break it off. He makes no effort to invite you out, once he's gotten enough information and attention from you, he departs with a "See you soon". You never meet up. You've realized he's terrible for you and don't pick up the phone when he calls you anymore.

Your dreams can be taken from you with this tactic. If they convince you that you need them for your talents to succeed it's similar to clipping a bird's wings. First you will feel demotivated, worthless, then weak, and eventually unable to practice your passions.

Instead of letting that happen, commit further to your callings. Find more people to work with, branch out, and learn how to do things yourself. Do anything that will fight off the atrophy of your abilities. Nothing stays the same, we're either getting better or getting worse. Invest in yourself so that you grow. The stronger you are the fewer people will be able to convince you that you need their help.

All of the narcissistic strategies come after your ability to nurture yourself. This is why self-care is the answer to their influence. After being exposed to them you will be convinced that taking care of yourself isn't a valid thing to spend your energy doing. They will rewire all of the resources that you have for yourself away from you through subterfuge and guilt. This is why you need to be firm in your own perspective and your own health. By being confident and responsible you cut off their access to you.

The targets that they want to manipulate are the ones that are weak. They don't want a fight, so they look for people prone to dependency issues. If you can find balance in your life then you won't look like someone who is prone to being responsive to their tactics. They seek out insecurities and self-doubt. By reaffirming yourself and being your own guide, you protect yourself from the bulk of their strategies.

Fixing insecurity is a difficult thing to do, but you don't need to do it all at once. In fact, the important part isn't to stop being insecure, but to stop projecting insecurity. It doesn't matter if you're insecure and no one knows, you're not making yourself a target. You have the right to feel however you do in your own head, although it's healthy to work on insecurities anyway. Learning how to project confidence is the necessary strategy, whether or not that confidence is legitimate. Stand up for yourself no matter how you feel about yourself. The action is the important part.

Law 18

«The Narcissist is Never at Fault, Their Surroundings Are»

The Law of Burdens

Have you gotten better since I've seen you?

One can see the image of the prodigal son in the narcissists, except the narcissists carries an incredibly toxic expectation. Instead of being risk-takers who need to be helped after failure, they often fall into being reckless while expecting you to clean up after them. Upon their return into your life, they will have expectations for your lifestyle, implying that you should measure up to certain standards that are never made clear. It is again an appraisal of your value and how much they can get out of knowing you.

They shift the guilt in their lives because they have no courage. When they are forced to face themselves, they find what they see so disgusting that they flee back into their fantasies of superiority. If they were to admit to their action then there would be no human standard that would excuse them. Even by their own morals they're disgusting once they appraise themselves honestly.

Because of this, while a narcissist is functioning, all things will be blamed on their victim. The responsibility will be on their supply to improve themselves and their situation. All of the actions in the world will be traced back to the supply because the narcissist needs a frame of reference in which they can lead their target through guilt and shaming.

The pleasure that they receive from this is one of the most warped dimensions of human emotions. It's sickening to observe and worse to be a part of. When there is a narcissistic parent and they target their children this behavior is especially toxic. The people that are supposed to guard their vulnerable offspring into the challenges of adulthood choose instead to whittle them down and infect them with serious mental anguish.

In romantic relationships this dynamic isn't much better. It turns love into responsibility of the worst kind. It turns you into the guardian of your lover. Now you need to care about how they're eating, how they feel, what their schedules are, everything that they should be able to do themselves. It's rare for a narcissist to grow up, and so one of the things that they need from their supply is the ability to handle adult responsibilities. Some even require their wives to buy their underwear.

This conditioning is ridiculous because narcissists flee from every concept of responsibility. They're not willing to accept any part of their own happiness or situation in life, their sense of entitlement prevents that. Instead of working to better their lives they think that they deserve better, which is a useless thought as they wait around, doing nothing but plotting on the happiness of others. There is no reason for anyone to do anything for them because narcissists have no interest in contributing back to society. As far as feeling goes, they're hollow. There is nothing that truly moves them other than advantage.

Everyone deserves better than to feed into this system. No one should think that they're the problem. No one knows better. We all get our own autonomy. If anyone has a different opinion then they are trying to herald back a return to feudalism. We killed our kings and they should stay dead, there is no benefit to a return to morality in which we thought there were lower and higher beings. No one deserves to be served, and no one should have to serve. Live your life for you. Better yourself for you.

Returning after seasons of absence, he asks you out to coffee. Out at the spot he asks about your painting career. You admit you've been too depressed to do anything but focus on work. He looks disappointed and stirs his drink, then chats about all of these projects he's been juggling. He tells grandiose stories that sound nothing but fantastic. It makes you feel embarrassed. You're not doing enough and you suspect him of exaggerating.

Still he's able to guilt you into a second date, then sleeping together. He comments that your cooking used to have a lighter touch to it. You roll your eyes. Your taste in music has stayed impeccable. All of the words sound hollow.

He appraises you like a doll, looking over your sides, testing your legs with his fingers. You can feel his eyes fixated on you. You can feel him smelling you. It's like being examined for sale. You feel unsafe, and start to plan on creating distance between him and your life.

Allowing them to have so much control over your life is letting someone else run your schedule. It's recreating the dynamics that a child has with an abusive parent, where someone else commands your time and actions. It'll leave you without the facilities needed to find your own pride and sense of pacing.

Get out of it by not letting their presence or absence in your life define your relationship with anything else. Keep the important parts of your life separate from the influence of anyone other than yourself for a while. Find what you want from what you're doing and never forget it.

The more you build up your life and stick to it the less room they will have to interrupt you. The bet that they make against you is that you won't have enough faith in yourself to stand up to them, so by listening to yourself and committing to yourself you will prove wrong their assumptions about you. Once you defend yourself, you're no longer an ideal form of supply.

They want you if you hate yourself, if you think that your dreams will lead nowhere, or if you're scared to stand up for yourself. They will flee from you if you're proud and self-affirming, and even before they do so, your quality of life will improve. There are nothing but good things ahead if you can commit to giving yourself the nurture that you need.

So remember that you can always be your own resource. Build up your spaces, take care of your appearance, and commit to your occupation. Spend your life on yourself so that you can reap the benefits of your own existence. Don't let someone else outsource the difficult parts of life to you. Struggle through them yourself and reap the rewards of your efforts.

Law 19

«Narcissists Will Insist on Loyalty and be Adverse to

Any Change»

The Law of Consistency

Thou shalt worship no idols before me.

With the storytelling that goes on in the narcissist's imagination, there come expectations. If you are a player in one of their games, then they expect you to remember that, to remember the rules of the game, the events that have gone on so far, and where the chips lay. If you manage to be on the same page as them then they see it as a form of loyalty, as a feature of yourself that defines you as one of their group.

If you cannot keep up with them, then they will suspect you of being an outsider. They will put you back into the category of normal people, taking away all of the attention that they used to give you. It will feel cold.

The narratives that form are complex. They create worlds in their imagination, perspectives on people, culture, religion, and everything, that they expect to be respected. Their political opinions start to become law. Their point of view becomes hegemonic. They do not tolerate disagreement.

This is because they don't want to share the spotlight. Their point of interacting with others is so that they can draw out supply from them. If someone else is getting attention then they are losing their objective. They want all the attention and effort to be directed towards them.

With this being an incredibly unhealthy balance in relationships, most people react poorly to it. Narcissists learn this over time and try to conceal how they manipulate people. Part of this is growing their victims' dependence on them, such as being involved in the way they think. If the narcissist can convince their target that he's smarter than them, then the narcissist can secure a place as a filter of informations for their victim.

By doing this they can grow their influence over the target until they get so much power over their lives that the target isn't able to process informations by themselves anymore. If the narcissist can successfully create this dynamic then it's easy for them to enforce loyalty because they are in control of so much of their victim's trust.

When a narcissist has this much power over their victim there are major risks. They can ruin opportunities for their target, grow panic disorders within them, and terrorize their lives. It is a terrifying position to be in and should be handled with care when ran into.

To guard against this, remember your feelings and your reactions. Don't let them explain your interpretation of life away. Listen to and consider their perspective, but if it doesn't correlate with yours then question it. It's normal for people to see things differently, but not so differently that it feels like someone is lying about how you felt or how you acted.

Rely on your instinct here. When someone is trying to force you into something you don't want to be anymore, or someone is relying on trust that you no longer have for them, it will make you feel weird. Your body will be aware that someone is trying to force you into unnatural behavior, that they're taking advantage of your trust. Listen to your discomfort and don't be pressured out of the way that you're reacting to life.

Once you respect that you're uncomfortable, take action to make yourself feel better. Take the space and resources you need to reestablish a healthy connection to the world around you. Don't be dragged down by pity or responsibility, don't let someone pressure their way back into your life. You have no responsibility but to live a life that you want to live. Embrace yourself and find what you need to do. Don't let narcissist make you forget you.

He comes back to you after a month of absence, using the key you gave to him. You don't even comment on him letting himself in, you just say hello. Within seconds he's speaking in indirect language, saying that the mission was going well, that you would soon be able to figure out the whole lifestyle thing. You can't even remember what he's talking about, but you do remember him being obsessed with some mission. Was it starting an e-commerce business? You ask him what he means when he brings up being able to move out into the country.

He rolls his eyes and sighs. It's what you want, he reminds you, it's what both of you want. You remember talking about it months ago, while you were in bed. The conversation was sort of mindless for you. You tell him that you have to keep working your way up your career, he freaks out and starts yelling. There's no way to calm the conversation. He storms out again, saying how he thought you were different. You have to live with it.

You can't be someone else's doll. Taste isn't transferrable, even though you may enjoy someone else's sense for it. Appreciation is good, but imitation usually isn't. It leaves you with weaker faculties, and inauthentic relationships with what you're trying to appreciate.

So instead, ignore the standards that are applied to you. We all have flaws and we all should work on them, but we don't need to obsess over them. Negativity isn't productive, it's defeatist.

Remember that you always have a right to ask questions, especially around decisions that someone else is encouraging you to make. Never go blindly into anything unless it is for someone you would trust with your life. Research and screening can prevent almost any issue from happening if you have enough respect for your own safety.

Stand up for yourself and make people earn your loyalty. Don't give out anything for free, it won't be respected. Either a narcissist will take it, or people won't trust it. Give out trust slowly, because character is revealed over time.

Law 20

«Without Giving What They Ask for, The Narcissist
Will Demand Forgiveness While Holding Grudges»

The Law of Forgiveness

Forgive me, for I am not forgiving.

The narcissist is not unfeeling. They do not feel for others. However, often they have a rich inner world of internal emotions, which is one of the most dangerous hooks for empaths. Narcissists provide a perspective of sensitivity for the self that empaths do not truly relate to, as empaths tend to be out of tune with the traditional idea of ego.

Due to this they understand some basic emotional principles, which boil down to things such as 'I feel shame and have made a mistake, so I desire forgiveness'. It is not uncommon for a narcissist to seek out forgiveness, but it is incredibly rare for them to extend it. They are the type of people to never forgive.

This is because they don't want your forgiveness, they want your permission. Perhaps they will admit they've been cheating on you and ask for you to take them back, but they will most likely cheat again. They don't respect boundaries. They want to be accepted after doing anything. In some cases, they may purposefully cross boundaries just to get a rise out of their target. This is because they feed off drama, it gives them entertainment and more information about people. They only see others as resources.

As an empath, another sort of HSP, or a human with a heart, it is difficult to turn away someone asking for forgiveness. No one wants to be harsh to someone groveling before them, there's something shameful about it. Narcissists know this and use it to their advantage, playing off their target's sense of social responsibility.

They want to leave you with a sense of being in the wrong, like you're being exceptionally cruel. Often it leaves the victim questioning their position. That's not because you need to take them back, that's because they're using your sense of feeling against you, knowing how to manipulate your good sense into trusting them again.

This is what makes the narcissist so dangerous. They've studied human behavior for years. They've learned our systems of communication like a play. They've become masters of eliciting expression from the people they're surrounded by. In the sneakiest ways they steal from the people who trust them, then convince their targets that they're responsible for their misfortune.

A single narcissist in your life can leave you completely imbalanced. You may start inscribing blame on yourself for things that couldn't possibly be your fault. They may blame you for things as trivial as traffic, economic events, or politics, things out of your control. If you start to take on these accusations then you will bear the weight of Jesus, carrying the shame of the entire species on your shoulders. That's a responsibility that's not for you.

If there is a network of narcissists in your life then your entire conception of reality may be at risk. It's hard enough to trace misinformation when there's one narcissist, if they have the advantage of having other manipulators to play with against you then it will be a situation that will not be able to be straightened. Be wary if your family is like this, but also be on guard if your spouse's family is like this.

Narcissists reinforce narcissists, that's why they prefer working within systems. Once a few of them are in communication then they can work on several targets, and with more success, because if they can get others to parrot what they spread then they can add legitimacy to it. While it may be possible to chase down a narcissist alone, to expose them to the truth about themselves and to cause their shame to no longer be repressed, it is impossible to nail down a narcissist while they are supported by their network. With their advantage in numbers, they will cling on to their perspectives and box out your efforts to unravel their constructed fables.

You're hanging out again. The last time it ended in a fight, you were screaming, he was saying awful things, but you decided to forgive him after he reached out to you. Lunch went well, except you kept catching things, little barbs in his words. Over time he mentioned the time you raised your voice, the time that fell to the ground crying, and the time that you struck his chest when he tried to hug you.

You mention that he had said awful things about your family and friends, that he had judged all of you as inferior and worthless people, but he brushes that off by getting angry. He says that you're ungrateful for how much he's trying and how much better he's being around you. You get quiet as he speaks faster and faster, louder and louder. The day is ruined.

His tantrum has replaced your expression, again. Through the intensity of his feeling he has redirected focus from the point that you were making. It always ends up centering on him. You cannot have problems.

Being around a standard like this will ruin your life. You will be trained that you and your intentions are bad and that you must succumb to the will of somebody outside yourself. It is turning you in an absolute source of supply for the narcissist. There will be nothing left to you but your thoughts, and even those one day might go quiet.

The best thing to do with a narcissist who engages in this is to stop associating with them. What you can gain from interacting with them is not worth the psychological trauma. You can go through every point with them meticulously, but the best you will achieve in doing this is making them realize the truth, thus exposing how pathetic they are to themselves. If you see that happen, it's an awful sight. Spare yourself.

Law 21

«What Will not Rule Itself Will be Taken by Lesser Forces»

The Law of Autonomy

What is a ship without a pilot?

Ultimately the narcissist is trying to apply inhuman standards and expectations to a very human world. In the modern era, we have completely done away with the moral arguments for slavery, but the narcissist does not seem to agree. They still think that they have the rights of the master, that they can command people and deserve to receive whatever they can from them. Truly like a virus, or a cancer, they will enter you and take over parts of you, breeding their own energy until you are completely worn out and incapable of being a good host.

They don't think you deserve what you have been given. In their mind, they could do more with what you have. If you trust them, then they will trickle poison into your psyche until they can control you. They will want to drive your social life, your health, your thoughts, and everything else they can access. When they do you will be subject to their rule, and they will be playing broker between you and the world.

This could mean anything. Maybe they will lead you into the life that you wanted, into success and friendships, but that's as likely as them killing you. When you're attached to a narcissist there is no way for you to plan your life. They keep your time and your resources continually in motion, never giving you the opportunity to settle your plans for yourself.

The reason why they won't let you find peace in your life is because they don't want to be your manager. They want to be your master. They don't want you to be able to move on, they don't want you to be strong, and they have no interest in your positive development other than to increase their own reputation.

When you don't have the right to choose your future then your brain will recoil. It's terrifying. You need to be able to predict your future, what you will be doing, and what you will do if things go wrong. Without security in answer to these concerns it is natural to feel anxious. This is a state of crisis because you can't promise your survival.

For the sake of your future and your health, address this. You cannot continue living under these standards without developing detrimental levels of stress. The human isn't meant to be enslaved. Don't give anyone permission to rule over your life.

With HSPs this dynamic will be incredibly dangerous. Their sensitivity and powerful internalization of their environment will leave them lost to the narcissist's encroachment of their inner world. All of the tactics of the narcissist target the social sensitivities that we have, such as insecurities, pity, and duty. Due to this HSPs are at risk because they are especially prone to be moved by such external stimuli.

In a dark twist, the HSP will also be incredibly valuable to the narcissist. The innate lack of defensiveness in the HSP will attract the narcissist because it means that they can rip out as much as they can take. They are the ideal victims for the narcissist's hunt.

So, for all of us who have suffered from narcissistic influence, empaths, HSPs, and people without heightened sensitivities, must find center and gain control over our own lives. We only have ourselves in our skin, and so we must tend to what we are given. The other option is to suffer, and there has been enough of that. Forgive yourself and give yourself better.

This journey will be terrifying to start because it will go everywhere, but stay brave. At the end of these travels is home, and along the path your soul will be found. All that was stolen can be returned.

He has opinions on your friends, on your work, on your school, on your habits, on everything. There's nothing you can do, nothing you can wear, nothing you can enjoy without critique. It makes you afraid to do anything around him; you have to download alternative messaging apps so he doesn't go through your life.

Everything starts an argument. Even your hobbies are no escape. It's an unlivable experience. You need some freedom. It can't keep going on like this. You file for divorce.

Unwelcome memories of your father start creeping in your thoughts. You remember those things he said about your dresses, the way he resented driving you to violin practice. You remember what it's like when someone treats you like a dead weight.

Part of you begins to believe that it's simply part of the human experience. This is how people choose to treat one another. It's part of the social contract. You carry his opinions and judgments without a fight because you've carried so many others before. It's natural to you, like loading a preset.

As things develop, you lose connection with your voice. Your thoughts get lost somewhere between your heart and your understanding. You look out the window on a sunny day and see fog. The neighborhood around you is near unrecognizable.

The goals that you had have been pushed to the side. He thinks they're trite. You don't need to be independent, you don't need to be recognized for your talent, and you don't need what you want. Again and again conversations drill this into you, leaving you defeated. This is because the narcissist wants you to crawl. Through your pain he expresses his majesty.

So years of your life are wasted like this, with someone pulling out pieces of what you need to survive as you try to understand their point of view. Their explanations will come out mixed and inconsistent, but they will insist, and by now you've forgotten the list of all of the changes in their stories. You are owed some sort of reason, just to be respected as an equal, but no true explanation is coming, they will never meet you where you are.

This is because you don't matter. In their world view you are a mere distraction from the essential focal point of life, them. There will never be a time where they stop and change their ways, so if you wait for it your carcass will be picked apart by their cold beaks as you apologize for the taste of your flesh.

Your entire future can be ruined by them because they attack your supply of time. They want the time that you need to develop yourself, to reach out to the world, and to invest in new hobbies. There is not a resource more precious than time, for it is the vessel of energy, and energy is what manifest all things. When you allow someone else to have influence in that domain then you have lost your control over your own potential.

A deep warning is given about the physical manifestations of suffering through an environment like this. It can cause residual headaches that never seem to go away, chronic pain, digestive issues, and other ailments. The body is only meant to handle so much stress. When you are living with a human parasite then you will suffer, and your body will not have the resources to repair itself.

This is not because there is anything wrong with you, this because the narcissist will always ask for too much. If they didn't, then we could attempt to help them. That is part of the tragedy.

Being exposed to someone trying to replace your sovereignty over your own life is one of the most dangerous circumstances for your energy. When there is a war for influence like that over you your life direction can easily be muddled and you may miss out from some of the most important opportunities in your life. This will happen because you were conditioned by someone who ultimately doesn't care about you, only the image of you.

Divorce, literal or metaphorical, is the best and most foolproof method when you're trying to combat this. You are not a ship. You are a pilot, just as every person is. If someone in your life believes otherwise, they cannot be a part of your life, because their entire purpose is to encroach upon other's sacred territory. The best defense is prevention, because they don't even deserve the opportunity to tear you down, or to continue doing so.

Let go of them and their standards, and then commit to a future which you want to inhabit. Communicate with yourself with positivity. You deserve to hear a supportive voice in your life, to feel proud in the things that you accomplish. If you struggle with dental hygiene then commit to brushing regularly, and feel good about when you remember to do so. Don't blame yourself if you can't hold up to your expectations, but be proud of the ones that you meet.

The more that you feed yourself positivity, the more distance you will be able to create from yourself and the influence of a narcissistic person. By creating and affirming a positive relationship between you and yourself you will be able to create a basis of strength in your life. Once you are able to manage that, branching out into life will come naturally.

Take time to invest in anything that you like. If baths bring you back to the world then take them regularly. If you're interested in old haikus, study them. Find anything that helps you appreciate your place in the world and solidify your relationship with it. Make sure to contribute positive energy to yourself as you would to anyone else, being sensitive and patient. The better that you are able to treat yourself the more you will be able to heal.

After you find balance within yourself your relationship with the world will straighten out. It will be easier for you to find the things that you want to commit to, and to enjoy the things that you aren't interested in as you pass them by. The world around you will no longer be off limits or unfamiliar, it will be something that you have reckoned with. It will be yours, as much as it is anybody else's.

Once you have reached harmony in this way you will be at an incredible place to start establishing boundaries. As you heal your sensitivities, your tastes, you're your opinions will return. You will be able to read warning signs. The more respect you give yourself, the more natural identifying where your boundaries are and keeping them up will become. This will happen subconsciously if you have healed your self-image, and so entering new relationships will be much less daunting. The more time that you spend establishing healthy archetypes the more your neurochemistry will be adapted to them.

This is why supporting yourself is so crucial. Studies have linked HSP with low serotonin and dopamine levels. Curiously they don't feel happiness as often, but they are more deeply affected by positive stimuli than other people. Everyone works this way on some level, so the process of loving yourself is crucial for all people, but for HSPs self-support may be the key in finding balance with the world around them. While recovering from narcissistic cohabitation there are no lengths that you should feel guilty about pursuing, provided they don't harm anyone else. Be your own best friend. You will beat up your bully.

Conclusion

Narcissists are some of the most difficult people to deal with. It is not an attitude, but a condition that they suffer from. In the DSM it is in placed in Cluster B personality disorders, the dramatic, emotional, and erratic cluster. It is important to note this when dealing with them, because they did not choose to be this way. They are not bad people. They are victims of their disorder, too. Most of them do not have malicious instincts, nor do they hate the people that they target, they just cannot conceive of the world in a different way. Many of them were exposed to these attitudes in childhood, and instead of learning their own model, they imitated what they were exposed to. It's a tragic situation.

That does not excuse their manipulation, or their sadistic tendencies. These laws contain the strategies of the narcissist when trying to manipulate you and your perspective, whether the narcissist is conscious of using these tactics or not. Internalize that you need to defend yourself and take care of your soul, and know that these laws reveal unhealthy dynamics that you cannot fix, but must discard.

The essential traits of their strategy are in gaslighting, projecting, guilt, duty, and image. They will always try to control narratives and aesthetics, insisting that they have a hand in how things are told or understand. These laws contain the ways of recognizing these, and several other tactics employed by narcissists in trying to control your life. If you can use these examples and apply them to your life with some creativity and honesty, you will see pathways to better standards and healthier relationships. Your narcissist isn't your person. You don't belong to anyone. You have a place in humanity. Join love instead of people who want to hide you.

Notes